Interactive Computing Series

Microsoft® Excel 2002 Brief Edition

Kenneth C. Laudon • Kenneth Rosenblatt

David Langley

Azimuth Interactive, Inc.

Boston   Burr Ridge, IL   Dubuque, IA   Madison, WI   New York   San Francisco   St. Louis
Bangkok   Bogotá   Caracas   Kuala Lumpur   Lisbon   London   Madrid   Mexico City
Milan   Montreal   New Delhi   Santiago   Seoul   Singapore   Sydney   Taipei   Toronto

McGraw-Hill Higher Education

A Division of The McGraw-Hill Companies

This book is printed on acid-free paper.

2 3 4 5 6 7 8 9 0 QPD/QPD 0 9 8 7 6 5 4 3 2

ISBN 0-07-247254-5

Publisher: *George Werthman*
Developmental editor I: *Sarah Wood*
Senior marketing manager: *Jeff Parr*
Senior project manager: *Pat Frederickson*
Senior production supervisor: *Michael R. McCormick*
Senior designer: *Pam Verros*
Supplement producer: *Mark Mattson*
Senior producer, Media technology: *David Barrick*
Cover design: *JoAnne Schopler*
Interior design: *Asylum Studios*
Cover photograph: *Bill Brooks/© Masterfile*
Compositor: *Azimuth Interactive, Inc.*
Typeface: *10/12 Times*
Printer: *Quebecor Printing Book Group/Dubuque*

Library of Congress Control Number: 2001092086

www.mhhe.com

InformationTechnology

Information Technology at McGraw-Hill/Irwin

At McGraw-Hill Higher Education, we publish instructional materials targeted at the higher education market. In an effort to expand the tools of higher learning, we publish texts, lab manuals, study guides, testing materials, software, and multimedia products.

At McGraw-Hill/Irwin (a division of McGraw-Hill Higher Education), we realize that technology has created and will continue to create new mediums for professors and students to use in managing resources and communicating information with one another. We strive to provide the most flexible and complete teaching and learning tools available as well as offer solutions to the changing world of teaching and learning.

MCGRAW-HILL/IRWIN IS DEDICATED TO PROVIDING THE TOOLS FOR TODAY'S INSTRUCTORS AND STUDENTS TO SUCCESSFULLY NAVIGATE THE WORLD OF INFORMATION TECHNOLOGY.

- **Seminar series**—Technology Connection seminar series offered across the country every year demonstrates the latest technology products and encourages collaboration among teaching professionals.

- **Osborne/McGraw-Hill**—This division of The McGraw-Hill Companies is known for its best-selling Internet titles: Harley Hahn's Internet & Web Yellow Pages, and the Internet Complete Reference. Osborne offers an additional resource for certification and has strategic publishing relationships with corporations such as Corel Corporation and America Online. For more information visit Osborne at www.osborne.com.

- **Digital solutions**—McGraw-Hill/Irwin is committed to publishing digital solutions. Taking your course online does not have to be a solitary venture, nor does it have to be a difficult one. We offer several solutions that will allow you to enjoy all the benefits of having course material online. For more information visit www.mhhe.com/solutions/index.mhtml.

- **Packaging options**—For more about our discount options, contact your local McGraw-Hill/Irwin Sales representative at 1-800-338-3987 or visit our Web site at www.mhhe.com/it.

Interactive Computing Series

GOALS/PHILOSOPHY

The *Interactive Computing Series* provides you with an illustrated interactive environment for learning software skills using Microsoft Office. The text uses both "hands-on" instruction, supplementary text, and independent exercises to enrich the learning experience.

APPROACH

The *Interactive Computing Series* is the visual interactive way to develop and apply software skills. This skills-based approach coupled with its highly visual, two-page spread design allows the student to focus on a single skill without having to turn the page. A Lesson Goal at the beginning of each lesson prepares the student to apply the skills with a real-world focus. The Quiz and Interactivity sections at the end of each lesson measure the student's understanding of the concepts and skills learned in the two-page spreads and reinforce the skills with additional exercises.

ABOUT THE BOOK

The **Interactive Computing Series** offers *two levels* of instruction. Each level builds upon the previous level.

Brief lab manual—covers the basics of the application, contains two to four chapters.

Introductory lab manual—includes the material in the Brief textbook plus two to four additional chapters. The Introductory lab manuals prepare students for the *Microsoft Office User Specialist Proficiency Exam (MOUS Certification)*.

Each lesson is divided into a number of Skills. Each **Skill** is first explained at the top of the page in the Concept. Each **Concept** is a concise description of why the Skill is useful and where it is commonly used. Each **Step (Do It!)** contains the instructions on how to complete the Skill. The appearance of the *MOUS Skill* icon on a Skill page indicates that the Skill contains instruction in at least one of the required MOUS objectives for the relevant exam. Though the icons appear in the Brief manuals as well as the Introductory manuals, only the Introductory manuals may be used in preparation for MOUS Certification.

Figure 1

| Skill: Each lesson is divided into a number of specific skills | **skill** | **Finding and Replacing Text** |

| Concept: A concise description of why the skill is useful and when it is commonly used | **concept** | The Find command enables you to search a document for individual occurrences of any word, phrase, or other unit of text. The Replace command enables you to replace one or all occurrences of a word that you have found. Together, the Find and Replace commands form powerful editing tools for making many document-wide changes in just seconds. |

| Do It!: Step-by-step directions show you how to use the skill in a real-world scenario | **do it !** | Use Find and Replace to spell a word consistently throughout a document. |

1. Open student file, wddoit12.doc, and save it as Report12.doc.

2. If necessary, place the insertion point at the beginning of the document. Word will search the document from the insertion point forward.

3. Click Edit, and then click Replace. The Find and Replace dialog box appears with the Replace tab in front and the insertion point in the Find What text box.

4. In the Find What box, type the two words per cent. Click in the Replace With box, and type the one word percent (see Figure 3-37).

5. Click Replace All to search the document for all instances of per cent and to replace them with percent. A message box appears to display the results. In this case, one replacement was made (see Figure 3-38). In short documents the Find and Replace procedure takes so little time that you usually cannot cancel it before it ends. However, in longer documents you can cancel a search in progress by pressing [Esc].

6. Click OK to close the message box. Click Close to close the Find and Replace dialog box.

7. Save and close the document, Report12.doc, with your change.

Hot Tips: Icons introduce helpful hints or trouble-shooting tips

| More: Provides in-depth information about the skill and related features | **more** | Clicking the Replace All button in the Find and Replace dialog box replaces every instance of the text you have placed in the Find What box. To examine and replace a word or phrase manually instead of automatically, start by clicking the Find Next button. If you desire to replace that instance, click the Replace button. |

Continue checking the document like this, clicking the Find Next button and then, if desired, the Replace button. Keep clicking the pairs of buttons until you have run through the entire document. Unless you absolutely must do otherwise, use the method for shorter documents only.

The first button under the Replace With box usually displays the word More. Click this button when you want to display the the Search Options area of the dialog box. With the area displayed, the More button converts to a Less button. Clicking on the Less button will hide the Search Options area. The Search drop-down list under Search Options determines the direction of the search relative to the insertion point. You can search upward or downward through the document or keep the Word default setting of All to check the whole document, including headers, footers, and footnotes. The Format drop-down list enables you to search criteria for fonts, paragraphs, tabs, and similar items. The Special drop-down list enables you to search for paragraph marks, tab characters, column breaks and related special characters. The No Formatting button removes all formatting criteria from searches. For information on the Search Option activated by the check boxes, consult Table 3-3.

The Find tab of the Find and Replace dialog box matches the Replace tab except it lacks the replace function and only searches documents for items that you specify.

In the book, each skill is described in a two-page graphical spread (Figure 1). The left side of the two-page spread describes the skill, the concept, and the steps needed to perform the skill. The right side of the spread uses screen shots to show you how the screen should look at key stages.

Figure 1 (cont'd)

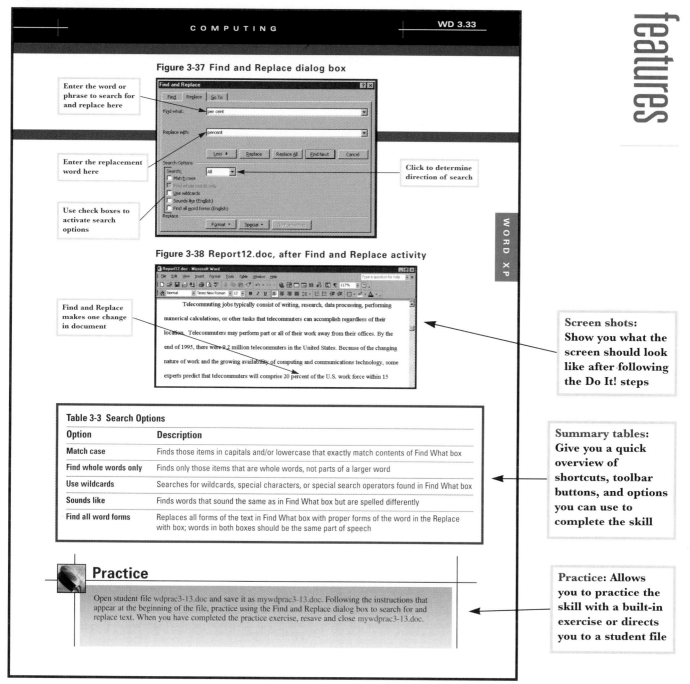

WD 3.33

COMPUTING

Figure 3-37 Find and Replace dialog box

Enter the word or phrase to search for and replace here

Enter the replacement word here

Click to determine direction of search

Use check boxes to activate search options

WORD XP

Figure 3-38 Report12.doc, after Find and Replace activity

Find and Replace makes one change in document

Telecommuting jobs typically consist of writing, research, data processing, performing numerical calculations, or other tasks that telecommuters can accomplish regardless of their location. Telecommuters may perform part or all of their work away from their offices. By the end of 1995, there were 9.2 million telecommuters in the United States. Because of the changing nature of work and the growing availability of computing and communications technology, some experts predict that telecommuters will comprise 20 percent of the U.S. work force within 15

Screen shots: Show you what the screen should look like after following the Do It! steps

Table 3-3 Search Options

Option	Description
Match case	Finds those items in capitals and/or lowercase that exactly match contents of Find What box
Find whole words only	Finds only those items that are whole words, not parts of a larger word
Use wildcards	Searches for wildcards, special characters, or special search operators found in Find What box
Sounds like	Finds words that sound the same as in Find What box but are spelled differently
Find all word forms	Replaces all forms of the text in Find What box with proper forms of the word in the Replace with box; words in both boxes should be the same part of speech

Summary tables: Give you a quick overview of shortcuts, toolbar buttons, and options you can use to complete the skill

Practice

Open student file wdprac3-13.doc and save it as mywdprac3-13.doc. Following the instructions that appear at the beginning of the file, practice using the Find and Replace dialog box to search for and replace text. When you have completed the practice exercise, resave and close mywdprac3-13.doc.

Practice: Allows you to practice the skill with a built-in exercise or directs you to a student file

END-OF-LESSON FEATURES

In the book, the learning in each lesson is reinforced at the end by a Quiz and a skills review called Interactivity, which provides step-by-step exercises and real-world problems for the students to solve independently.

The following is a list of supplemental material available with the Interactive Computing Series:

Skills Assessment

SimNet eXPert (Simulated Network Assessment Product)—SimNet provides a way for you to test students' software skills in a simulated environment. SimNet is available for Microsoft Office 97, Microsoft Office 2000, and Microsoft Office XP. SimNet provides flexibility for you in your course by offering:

- Pre-testing options
- Post-testing options
- Course placement testing
- Diagnostic capabilities to reinforce skills
- Proficiency testing to measure skills
- Web or LAN delivery of tests
- Computer based training materials (New for Office XP)
- MOUS preparation exams
- Learning verification reports
- Spanish Version

Instructor's Resource Kits

The Instructor's Resource Kit provides professors with all of the ancillary material needed to teach a course. McGraw-Hill/Irwin is dedicated to providing instructors with the most effective instruction resources available. Many of these resources are available at our Information Technology Supersite www.mhhe.com/it. Our Instructor's Kits are available on CD-ROM and contain the following:

Diploma by Brownstone—is the most flexible, powerful, and easy-to-use computerized testing system available in higher education. The diploma system allows professors to create an Exam as a printed version, as a LAN-based Online version, and as an Internet version. Diploma includes grade book features, which automate the entire testing process.

Instructor's Manual—Includes:
–Solutions to all lessons and end-of-unit material
–Teaching Tips
–Teaching Strategies
–Additional exercises

PowerPoint Slides—NEW to the *Interactive Computing Series*, all of the figures from the application textbooks are available in PowerPoint slides for presentation purposes.

Student Data Files—To use the *Interactive Computing Series*, students must have Student Data Files to complete practice and test sessions. The instructor and students using this text in classes are granted the right to post the student files on any network or stand-alone computer, or to distribute the files on individual diskettes. The student files may be downloaded from our IT Supersite at www.mhhe.com/it.

Series Web Site—Available at www.mhhe.com/cit/apps/laudon.

Digital Solutions

Pageout—is our Course Web site Development Center. Pageout offers a Syllabus page, Web site address, Online Learning Center Content, online exercises and quizzes, gradebook, discussion board, an area for students to build their own Web pages, and all the features of Pageout Lite. For more information please visit the Pageout Web site at www.mhla.net/pageout.

Digital Solutions (continued)

OLC/Series Web Sites—Online Learning Centers (OLCs)/Series Sites are accessible through our Supersite at www.mhhe.com/it. Our Online Learning Centers/Series Sites provide pedagogical features and supplements for our titles online. Students can point and click their way to key terms, learning objectives, chapter overviews, PowerPoint slides, exercises, and Web links.

The McGraw-Hill Learning Architecture (MHLA)—is a complete course delivery system. MHLA gives professors ownership in the way digital content is presented to the class through online quizzing, student collaboration, course administration, and content management. For a walk-through of MHLA visit the MHLA Web site at www.mhla.net.

Packaging Options—For more about our discount options, contact your local McGraw-Hill/Irwin Sales representative at 1-800-338-3987 or visit our Web site at www.mhhe.com/it.

Visit www.mhhe.com/it
THE ONLY SITE WITH ALL YOUR CIT AND MIS NEEDS.

acknowledgments

The *Interactive Computing Series* is a cooperative effort of many individuals, each contributing to an overall team effort. The Interactive Computing team is composed of instructional designers, writers, multimedia designers, graphic artists, and programmers. Our goal is to provide you and your instructor with the most powerful and enjoyable learning environment using both traditional text and interactive techniques. Interactive Computing is tested rigorously prior to publication.

Our special thanks to George Werthman, our Publisher; Sarah Wood, our Developmental Editor; and Jeffrey Parr, Marketing Director for Computer Information Systems. They have provided exceptional market awareness and understanding, along with enthusiasm and support for the project, and have inspired us all to work closely together. In addition, Steven Schuetz provided valuable technical review of our interactive versions, and Charles Pelto contributed superb quality assurance.

The Azimuth team members who contributed to the *Interactive Computing Series* are:

Ken Rosenblatt (Editorial Director, Writer)
Russell Polo (Technical Director)
Robin Pickering (Developmental Editor, Writer)
David Langley (Writer)
Chris Hahnenberger (Multimedia Designer)

Interactive Computing Series

Microsoft® Excel 2002 Brief Edition

contents

Excel 2002 Brief Edition

Preface	**v**
LESSON ONE	
Introduction to Spreadsheet Software	**EX 1.1**
Introducing Excel and Worksheet Design	EX 1.2
Starting Excel	EX 1.4
Exploring the Excel Window	EX 1.6
Moving Around the Worksheet ⑤	EX 1.10
Entering Labels ⑤	EX 1.14
Saving and Closing a Workbook ⑤	EX 1.16
Opening a Workbook ⑤	EX 1.20
Editing a Cell's Information ⑤	EX 1.22
Using the Office Assistant	EX 1.24
Other Excel Help Features	EX 1.26
Shortcuts	EX 1.28
Quiz	EX 1.29
Interactivity	EX 1.31
LESSON TWO	
Manipulating Data in a Worksheet	**EX 2.1**
Cutting, Copying, and Pasting Labels ⑤	EX 2.2
Entering Values ⑤	EX 2.4
Entering Formulas ⑤	EX 2.6
Using Functions ⑤	EX 2.8
Using the Insert Function Feature ⑤	EX 2.10
Copying and Pasting Formulas	EX 2.12
Using What-If Analysis	EX 2.16
Previewing and Printing a Worksheet	EX 2.20
Shortcuts	EX 2.22
Quiz	EX 2.23
Interactivity	EX 2.25

⑤ Skill covers at least one MOUS Certification objective.

Excel 2002 continued

LESSON THREE

3

Formatting Worksheet Elements — EX 3.1

Merging and Splitting Cells ⑨	EX 3.2
Formatting Cell Labels ⑨	EX 3.4
Formatting Cell Values ⑨	EX 3.6
Formatting Rows and Columns ⑨	EX 3.8
Inserting and Deleting Rows and Columns ⑨	EX 3.10
Hiding, Unhiding, and Protecting Cells ⑨	EX 3.12
Defining and Naming Cell Ranges ⑨	EX 3.16
Filling a Cell Range with Labels	EX 3.18
Applying Shading, Patterns, and Borders to Cells & Ranges	EX 3.20
Applying AutoFormat to a Worksheet ⑨	EX 3.22
Shortcuts	EX 3.24
Quiz	EX 3.25
Interactivity	EX 3.27

LESSON FOUR

4

Inserting Objects and Charts — EX 4.1

Inserting Text Objects ⑨	EX 4.2
Enhancing Graphics ⑨	EX 4.4
Adding and Editing Comments ⑨	EX 4.6
Understanding Excel Charts	EX 4.8
Creating a Chart ⑨	EX 4.10
Moving and Resizing a Chart ⑨	EX 4.14
Formatting a Chart ⑨	EX 4.16
Changing a Chart's Type ⑨	EX 4.18
Using Advanced Printing Features	EX 4.20
Shortcuts	EX 4.22
Quiz	EX 4.23
Interactivity	EX 4.25

Glossary	**EX 1**
Index	**EX 9**
File Directory	**EX 12**

⑨ Skill covers at least one MOUS Certification objective.

Introduction to Spreadsheet Software

Excel 2002

Microsoft Excel 2002 is a computer application that facilitates your ability to organize and record data, and then extract results from the data. With Excel, you can enter text labels and numerical values into an electronic spreadsheet, which is a grid made up of columns and rows. Just like a handwritten ledger that might be used for bookkeeping or accounting, an electronic spreadsheet consists of individual worksheets that enable you to record distinct, but related, data in a common location.

Being able to use spreadsheet software can help you both professionally and personally. By providing an organized structure in which to work, Excel can increase the efficiency with which you conduct business and manage your own affairs. Excel's ability to perform and automate calculations saves you time and decreases the possibility of human error compromising the integrity of your work.

An Excel spreadsheet is nearly as versatile as a blank canvas. Businesses use spreadsheets to plan budgets, track expenses and profits, and project future values of prices and transactions. A worksheet could also be used to lay out a schedule or a record of customers. As you work with Excel, you will find that any task that involves organizing information may be well served by the spreadsheet format.

Using Excel, you will learn how to create a spreadsheet employing proper design techniques. You then will explore the fundamentals of the application and become familiar with its basic elements and operations. Later on, some of Excel's more advanced features, such as formulas, What-If analysis, and charts will broaden your ability to manipulate data in a spreadsheet. If you need assistance while using Excel, the program includes an extensive Help facility, as well as direct links to online support via the World Wide Web.

Lesson Goal:

Learn the basics of Excel as you begin to construct a worksheet that will track the income, expenses, and profits of a business.

- Introducing Excel and Worksheet Design
- Starting Excel
- Exploring the Excel Window
- Moving Around the Worksheet
- Entering Labels
- Saving and Closing a Workbook
- Opening a Workbook
- Editing a Cell's Information
- Using the Office Assistant
- Other Excel Help Features
- Exiting Excel

skill

Introducing Excel and Worksheet Design

concept

Microsoft Excel is an electronic spreadsheet application designed to make the creation and use of professional-quality spreadsheets fast and easy. A spreadsheet is a table composed of rows and columns that stores text and numbers for easy viewing and tabulation. The intersection of a row and column creates a unit called a cell, in which you can enter data. Electronic spreadsheets are very useful for performing rapid and accurate calculations on groups of interrelated numbers. Using Excel, you can:

- Organize information rapidly and accurately. With the proper data and formulas, Excel calculates your results automatically.

- Recalculate automatically. Fixing errors in Excel is easy. When you find a mistake and correct the entry, Excel recalculates all related data automatically.

- Keep track of the effect that changing one piece of data has on related numbers. You can guess changes that may occur in the future and see how they could change the results of your calculations—a feature called What-If analysis.

- Display data as graphs or charts. Excel enables you to display numeric data graphically in the form of charts that are updated automatically as the data on which they are based change. For example, Figure 1-1 shows the data in a spreadsheet also displayed in the form of a pie chart. Charts are often easier to read than raw data and make the relationships among data easier to understand. ⬛ If your copy of Excel has been used previously, the appearance of the application window may differ from the one shown in the figure because another user may have resized the window or customized the screen.

A spreadsheet's organization is shaped by the goal or purpose of the data. A well-designed spreadsheet should be accurate and easily understood. Toward that end, you may choose to design your spreadsheets using the four distinct sections visible in Figure 1-2: documentation, assumptions, input, and results.

- The documentation section consists of a complete description of the name of the author, the purpose of the spreadsheet, the date it was created, and the name of the spreadsheet file. Documentation also should detail the use of named cell ranges and macros. Ranges are blocks of cells that contain similar or related data, or are acted upon as a single unit. Macros are sets of programming instructions that automate spreadsheet tasks.

- The assumptions section displays variable factors that may change in a worksheet. For example, a profit projection might assume that sales will increase by 10 percent each quarter. If the assumption is changed, or turns out to be an inaccurate projection, the amount of profit changes accordingly. If you document an assumption, it is much easier to change it later. Assumptions are useful when conducting a What-If analysis, which calculates the effects of changes in a spreadsheet. For instance, what if sales only grow by 5 percent instead of 10 percent?

- The input section of a spreadsheet stores the data that you enter and manipulate. In Figure 1-2, the input section contains data for income and expenditures. Input data are generally arranged in blocks of numbers organized Spin columns and rows.

- The results, or output section displays the outcome of the calculations performed on the input data. Output data are generally placed below or to the right of input data.

more

An Excel file is also known as a workbook. Excel stores each workbook you create as an individual file in your computer's memory. A workbook file can be a single worksheet or may contain many pages of data and charts. Each file should have a unique name so that you can differentiate it from other files. Excel files use the file extension .xls. A file extension is (generally) a three-character code separated from the file name with a period, pronounced "dot," that tells the computer what application is associated with a particular file and what type of data the file contains. When saving workbook files, you should avoid using additional periods in file names and changing the .xls extension. If you change the extension, Excel may no longer recognize your workbook files and may not be able to open them.

Figure 1-1 Worksheet made with Microsoft Excel

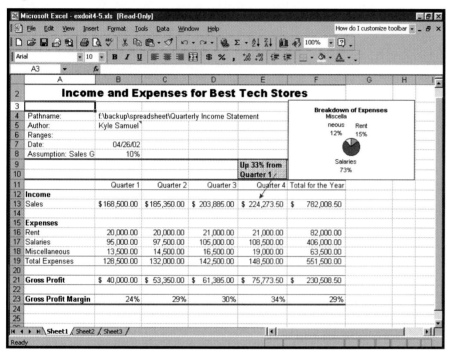

Figure 1-2 Organization of a spreadsheet

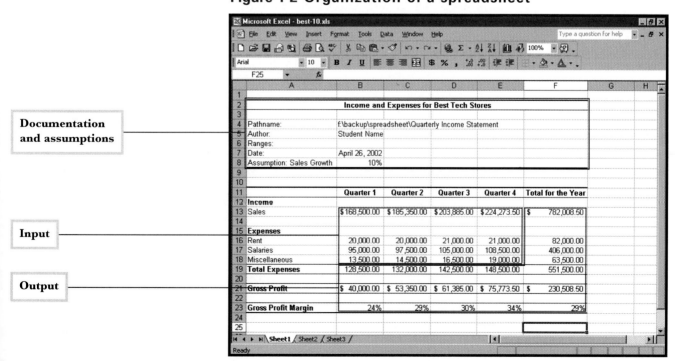

Documentation and assumptions

Input

Output

skill | Starting Excel

concept

The first step in using the Microsoft Excel program, or application, is launching it. The Windows operating system provides a number of ways to launch programs. When you install Excel (or Microsoft Office, the suite of programs of which Excel is a part), a shortcut to the program is placed on the Windows Start menu automatically. You can also open Excel by locating and running its executable file, named Excel.exe, through My Computer or Windows Explorer.

do it !

Use the Start menu to launch the Microsoft Excel application.

1. Turn on your computer and monitor and make sure that any peripheral devices such as your mouse are connected properly. When your edition of the Windows operating system finishes loading, the Windows desktop should appear on your screen (you may be asked to provide a user name and password before Windows finishes loading).

2. Click the Start button [Start] on the Windows taskbar, which generally is located at the bottom of the screen. The Windows Start menu will appear.

3. Move the mouse pointer ↖ up the Start menu to the Programs folder. The Programs sub-menu will open beside the Start menu.

4. Move the mouse pointer over to the Programs submenu from the Start menu, and rest the pointer over Microsoft Excel. The program name will be highlighted, as shown in Figure 1-3. Newer editions of the Windows operating system such as Windows Me utilize personalized menus, which means that only the items you use most frequently are displayed on a menu when it first opens. If personalized menus are active on your computer and you do not see Microsoft Excel listed on the Programs menu, click the double arrow at the bottom of the menu to display the rest of the program listings. It is also possible that the program will be listed on another submenu of the Start menu.

5. Click the left mouse button once. Excel will open with a blank workbook in the window (see Figure 1-4). If your copy of Excel has been used previously, the appearance of the application window may differ from the one shown in the figure.

more

Do not be alarmed if your desktop or Start menu do not match the descriptions above or the figures on the next page exactly. With several different versions of Windows and countless software applications available, variances in system configuration are more than likely. Windows itself is highly customizable, so the location or appearance of items such as the taskbar and the desktop are also subject to change. Furthermore, you can customize the way in which you interact with the operating system. For example, you can alter the functionality of the mouse so that tasks that normally require a double-click only require a single click. For the purposes of this book, the term click means to press and release the left mouse button quickly. When instructed to double-click, you should press and release the left mouse button twice in rapid succession. A right-click instruction requires you to press and release the right mouse button once. Finally, drag means to press and hold the left mouse button down, move the mouse as instructed, and then release the mouse button at the appropriate point to complete the action.

Figure 1-3 Opening Excel from the Start menu

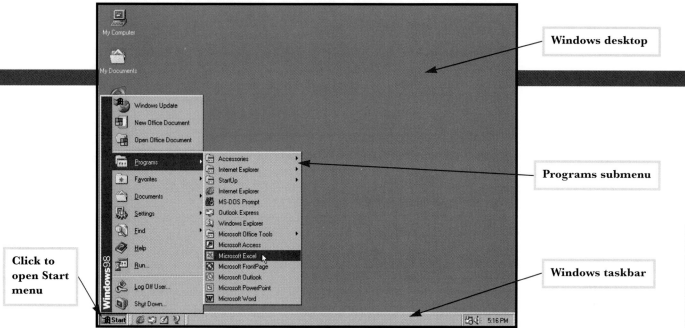

Windows desktop

Programs submenu

Click to open Start menu

Windows taskbar

Figure 1-4 Excel application window

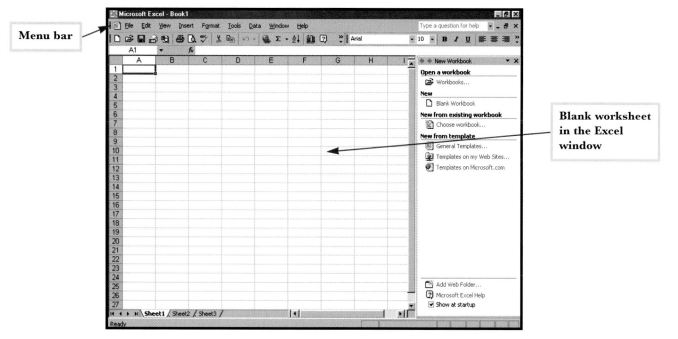

Menu bar

Blank worksheet in the Excel window

Practice

Click the File menu title on the Menu bar. The File menu will drop down below its menu title. Move the mouse pointer down the File menu and click the Exit command to close the Excel application. If you do not see the Exit command, click the double arrow at the bottom of the menu to expand the menu. When you have successfully exited Excel, use the Start menu to open the application again.

skill | Exploring the Excel Window

concept

In order to begin building a spreadsheet, it is necessary to become familiar with the Excel window and worksheet elements. The Excel application window consists of many features that are common to most applications running under the Windows operating system. These include a Title bar, Menu bar, document (worksheet) window and window control buttons, and toolbars. In addition to these items, Excel has many unique features that are designed to make worksheet production fast, flexible, and convenient.

do it !

Familiarize yourself with the Excel screen by examining various features.

1. Start Excel if the application is not already running. If the Excel window does not fill the screen, click the Maximize button ▣ on the right edge of the Title bar. The Title bar at the top of the window displays the name of the program and the name of the file that is active. When Excel opens, it automatically creates a new workbook containing three blank worksheets that is called Book1 (subsequent new files opened during the same work session are called Book2, Book3, and so on). The Title bar also houses the Minimize ▬, Maximize ▣ or Restore ▣, and Close buttons ✕, which are used to control the window. The Minimize button reduces the window to a program button on the taskbar. The Maximize button appears when the Excel window does not fill the entire screen. When the window is maximized, the Restore button, which returns the window to its previous size and location, appears in place of the Maximize button. ◥ Notice that a second set of control buttons appears just below the set on the Title bar. This second set of buttons applies to the active workbook file, not the entire application window, making it easier to work with multiple open Excel files at once. If you minimize the active file, it is reduced to a small Title bar at the bottom of the application window.

2. The Menu bar displays the titles of the menus containing Excel commands. Click File on the Menu bar to open the File menu. Excel 2002 uses personalized menus by default, so only a few commands may appear when you first open a menu. If you do not click one of the available commands, the menu will expand after a few seconds to reveal more commands. You can expedite this expansion by clicking the double arrow at the bottom of the menu or by clicking the menu title again. Alternatively, double-click the menu title to open the full menu right away. As you use Excel more and more, the program learns which commands you use most often. These commands will then be the first to appear when you open a menu. Click File again to close the File menu.

3. The Standard toolbar contains buttons that serve as shortcuts to commonly used commands. Move the mouse pointer over the New button ▯ on the Standard toolbar. A brief description of the button's function, called a ScreenTip, will appear. Guide the mouse pointer over the toolbars, pausing on each button to read its description, as shown in Figure 1-5. Next to the Standard toolbar in the same row in the default Excel setup is the Formatting toolbar, which contains buttons for formatting text, inserted objects, and the structure of the worksheet. ◥ The Standard and Formatting toolbars are just two of the many toolbars available in Excel. To activate additional toolbars, open the View menu from the Menu bar and point to the Toolbars command. A submenu of toolbar names will appear. Click a toolbar name to activate it, as shown in Figure 1-6.

(continued on EX 1.8)

Figure 1-5 Elements of the application window

Title bar

Menu bar

Standard toolbar

ScreenTip

Active worksheet in workbook window

Formatting toolbar

Task Pane: new feature in Excel 2002 that organizes related commands in one easy-to-reach location

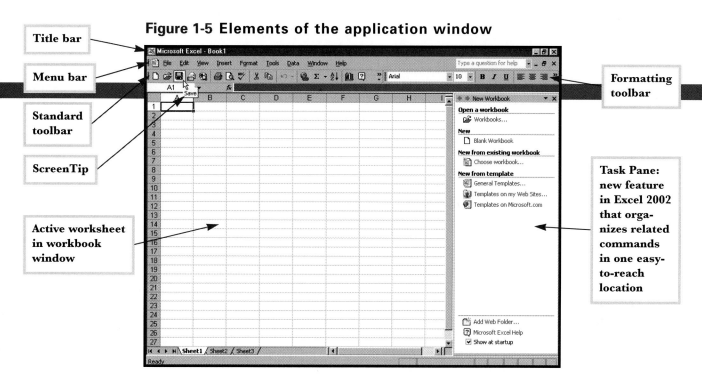

Figure 1-6 Activating toolbars

Check mark indicates an active item; click to deactivate

Toolbars submenu

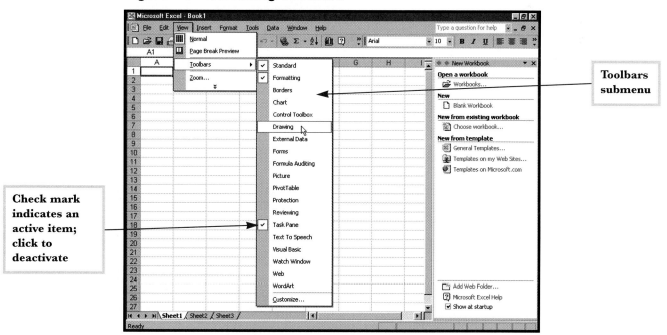

skill Exploring the Excel Window (cont'd)

do it!

4. Click the letter A that heads the first column of the worksheet. Column A becomes high-lighted indicating that it is selected, as shown in Figure 1-7. Columns in a worksheet are designated by letters, from A to Z, then AA to AZ, and so on up to IV for a total of 256 columns.

5. Click the number 1 at the left end of the first row. Row 1 becomes highlighted indicating that it is selected. Rows are labeled numerically down the left side of the worksheet from 1 to 65,536.

6. Click the space at the intersection of column D and row 7. The intersection of a row and a column is called a cell. A cell name, or address, consists of its column letter and row number. Cell D7 is now active. Excel indicates the active cell by surrounding it with a dark rectangle called the cell pointer. When a cell is active, you can enter new data into it or edit any data that are already there. You can make another cell active by clicking it, or by moving the cell pointer with the arrow keys on the keyboard.

7. Click cell F12. The Name box displays the address of the active cell.

8. Double-click cell F12. An insertion point appears in the cell and the pointer changes to an I-beam (see Figure 1-8). At the bottom of the Excel window, the text in the Status bar changes from Ready to Enter, indicating that you can enter or edit labels, values, or for-mulas. The Status bar provides feedback on your current activity in Excel and displays the status of particular keys such as the Caps Lock key. ◆ You can enter data in an active cell without double-clicking it, but any data already there will be erased immediately.

9. Click the down arrow on the vertical scroll bar on the right side of the worksheet to move the sheet down one row, hiding row 1. The vertical scroll bar and the horizontal scroll bar on the lower edge of the worksheet help you move quickly around the worksheet.

10. Below the active worksheet, Excel provides Sheet tabs that you can click to switch to other worksheets in the active workbook. Click the Sheet2 tab. Notice that the cell pointer moves from cell F12, the active cell on Sheet1, to cell A1, the active cell on Sheet2. The Sheet tabs enable you to organize related worksheets in a single workbook. Workbooks may contain up to 255 worksheets. Sheet tab scrolling buttons (in the lower-left corner of the window) allow you to view Sheet tabs that are hidden. Click the Sheet1 tab.

more

Standard scroll bars offer four basic ways of navigating. Clicking the arrows on either end of a scroll bar moves the worksheet view in small increments. The position of the scroll bar box relative to the ends of the scroll bar gives you an indication of where you are in the worksheet. To move in larger increments, click the scroll bar itself on either side of the scroll bar box. To move in even larger increments, drag the scroll bar box in the direction you want to move. Since Excel worksheets can grow quite lengthy, you also can hold down the [Shift] key on the keyboard while dragging the scroll bar box to advance rapidly through large portions of a worksheet. Be careful when using these last two methods, however, because scrolling by dragging is much less precise than scrolling by clicking.

As noted on the previous page, the Task Pane is a feature in Excel 2002 that brings together common, related commands in a convenient location. The Task Pane is context-sensitive, meaning that it changes according to the actions you perform. The Task Pane may be activated and deactivated just like a toolbar. The application and document control icons (see Figure 1-8) at the left end of the Title bar and Menu bar, respectively, offer menus containing the Close, Minimize, Maximize, and Restore commands.

Excel 2002

Figure 1-7 Selecting a column

Column A heading button

Name box

Row 1 heading button

Cell D7

Task Pane

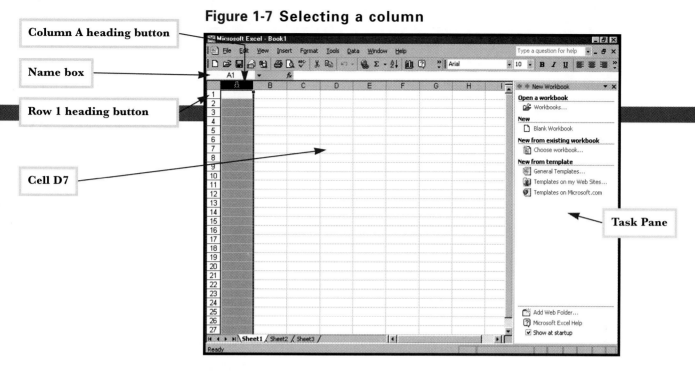

Figure 1-8 Working in an active cell

Control menu icons

Cell pointer

Sheet tabs

Sheet tab scrolling buttons

Insertion point: indicates where text will be entered

I-beam: allows you to place insertion point accurately

Vertical scroll bar

Horizontal scroll bar

Status bar

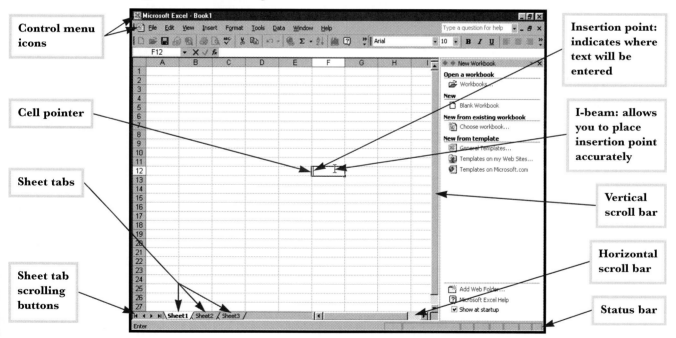

Practice

As shown in the preceding figures, the Standard and Formatting toolbars are arranged in a single row. This setting gives you more screen space, but limits the number of buttons you can see on each of the toolbars. The double arrow pointing to the right at the end of a toolbar indicates that more buttons are available. The downward-pointing arrow indicates that a menu will appear if you click the arrows. Click a set of arrows and then click Show Buttons on Two Rows. The Formatting toolbar will move below the Standard toolbar so you have better access to the buttons on both toolbars. When the buttons are shown on two rows, the command you clicked will appear as Show Buttons on One Row.

skill

Moving Around the Worksheet

concept

To use Excel effectively, you must be able to maneuver between cells in the workspace. To do this, you may use either the mouse or the keyboard depending on your personal preference or the task you are trying to accomplish. For example, if you are entering a large quantity of data quickly into cells that are close together, it may be easier and more efficient to use the keyboard. If you need to select a cell that is far from the active cell, using the mouse probably would be more effective.

do it !

Move to various points on a worksheet to familiarize yourself with Excel's navigation.

1. If Excel is not already running, start the application so you are working with a blank worksheet (if Excel is running, you should be on Sheet1).

2. Using the mouse, move the mouse pointer ✛ to cell B4 and click the left mouse button. The cell becomes surrounded by a heavy border, as shown in Figure 1-9, marking it as the active cell.

3. Press [◄—] on the keyboard. The cell pointer moves over one cell to the left to A4.

4. Press [▲] on the keyboard. The cell pointer moves up one cell to A3.

5. Press [—►] and then [▼] to return the cell pointer to cell B4.

6. Click once on the arrow at the right end of the horizontal scroll bar. The worksheet scrolls to the left so that a column further to the right is visible.

7. Scroll down one row by clicking once on the arrow at the bottom of the vertical scroll bar.

8. Click the arrow on the right end of the horizontal scroll button until column Z is visible. Notice that the scroll bar box shrinks to allow you a larger movement area, as seen in Figure 1-10.

9. Click and hold the mouse button on the horizontal scroll bar box. Drag the box to the left until you can see column A, and then release the mouse button.

(continued on EX 1.12)

Figure 1-9 Cell B4 active

Standard and Formatting toolbars now occupy two rows (see Practice on page EX 1.9)

Mouse pointer appears as a thick cross when over the worksheet

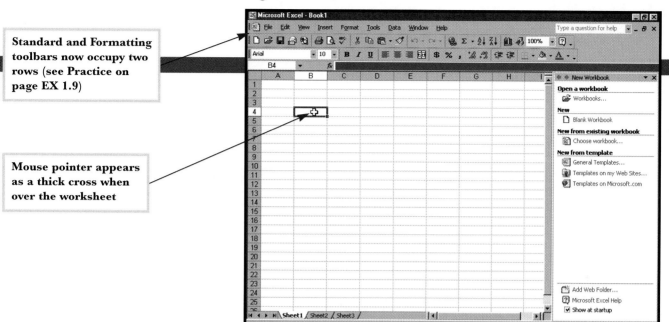

Figure 1-10 Scrolling through a worksheet

Name box still displays active cell, B4, even though it is no longer visible

Row 4 button highlighted, indicating that a cell in that row is selected

Column names extend past Z and begin again with AA, AB, and so on

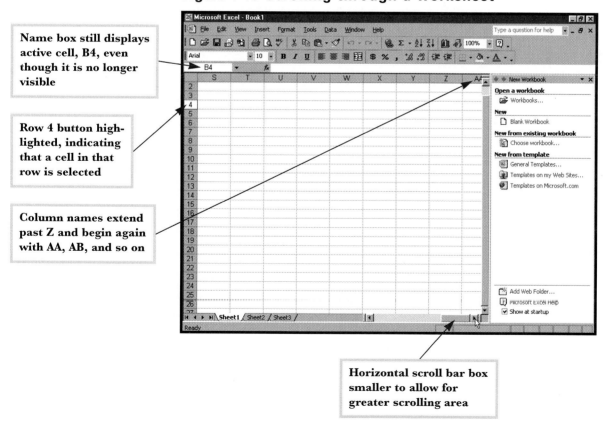

Horizontal scroll bar box smaller to allow for greater scrolling area

skill Moving Around the Worksheet (cont'd)

do it !

10. Click Edit on the Menu bar, then click the Go To command. The Go To dialog box appears. The Go To dialog box enables you to go to a part of the worksheet to which it would not be convenient to scroll. ◆ If you do not see the Go To command on the Edit menu, click the double arrow at the bottom of the menu to reveal more commands. You also can open the Go To dialog box by pressing the keyboard shortcut [Ctrl]+[G].

11. Type E2002 in the text box labeled Reference at the bottom of the dialog box, as shown in Figure 1-11 (it is not necessary to click in the box first—the blinking insertion point indicates that the text box is ready to receive text). You may type the cell reference using lowercase or uppercase letters. Excel will convert the letters to uppercase automatically.

12. Click the OK button [OK]. Excel immediately moves the cell pointer to the cell you referenced in the Go To dialog box, E2002.

13. Press [Ctrl]+[Home] (while holding down the [Ctrl] key, press the [Home] key). This keyboard shortcut moves the cell pointer to the beginning of the worksheet, cell A1. Some of the more common methods of moving around a worksheet are summarized in Table 1-1. ◆ To move across a large area of blank cells, press [End] on the keyboard. The word END will appear in the Status bar. Then press an arrow key. The cell pointer will jump to the next filled cell in the direction of the arrow key you pressed.

more

As you have learned, a workbook can be made up of many worksheets. The Sheet tabs at the bottom of the worksheet, labeled Sheet1, Sheet2, and Sheet3 by default, enable you to view the different worksheets within a workbook. You can keep interrelated data across multiple worksheets in the same workbook for viewing, cross referencing, and calculation. To add a blank worksheet to a workbook, select the Worksheet command from the Insert menu. The tab for the new worksheet will appear in front of the tab for the active worksheet.

You can change the order in which a Sheet tab appears in the row of tabs by dragging it to a new position. The mouse pointer will appear with a blank sheet icon attached to it ⬚ while you are dragging a tab, and a small arrow will indicate where the tab will be placed when you release the mouse button. The tab scrolling buttons |◄ ◄ ► ►|, located to the left of the Sheet tabs, allow you to view tabs that do not fit in the window. Clicking one of the outer buttons moves you to the first or last tab, while clicking one of the inner buttons moves you through the tabs one at a time. The tab scrolling buttons only function when enough worksheets have been added to the workbook to cause some of the tabs to be hidden.

If you right-click the tab scrolling buttons, a shortcut menu listing all of the worksheets in your workbook will appear. Simply click the name of the worksheet you want to view to display it. You can rename a worksheet by double-clicking its tab and then editing the name like normal text. Right-clicking a tab opens a shortcut menu with commands that enable you to rename, delete, insert, and copy or move a worksheet, or change the color of the tab.

Figure 1-11 Go To dialog box

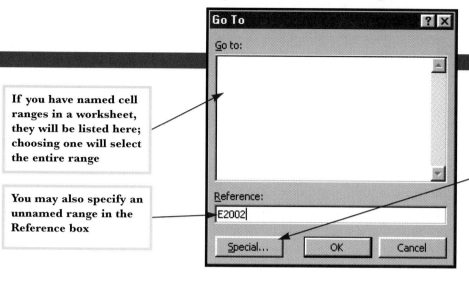

If you have named cell ranges in a worksheet, they will be listed here; choosing one will select the entire range

Click the Special button to go to items in the worksheet other than cells such as formulas, inserted objects, and comments

You may also specify an unnamed range in the Reference box

Excel 2002

Table 1-1 Moving in a worksheet

Movement	Action
Left one cell	Press [◄—] or [Shift]+[Tab]
Right one cell	Press [—►] or [Tab]
Up one cell	Press [▲] or [Shift]+[Enter]
Down one cell	Press [▼] or [Enter] (in default setup)
Left one column or right one column	Click the left arrow or right arrow on the horizontal scroll bar
Up one row or down one row	Click the up arrow or down arrow on the vertical scroll bar
Up one screen or down one screen	Press [Page Up] or [Page Down]
Left one screen or right one screen	Press [Alt]+[Page Up] or [Alt]+[Page Down]
Go to cell A1	[Ctrl]+[Home]
Go to column A in current row	[Home]

Practice

Click cell E12 to make it active, then use the arrow keys to move the cell pointer to G7. Open the Go To dialog box and navigate to cell CH10514. Finally move the cell pointer to cell A1.

skill **Entering Labels**

concept

Labels are used to annotate and describe the data you place into rows and columns on a worksheet. Properly labeled data make your spreadsheet easy to understand and interpret. Labels can consist of text or numbers and are aligned to the left of the cell to differentiate them from data used in calculations. Excel left-aligns labels for you automatically. You should enter labels into your spreadsheet first so that your rows and columns are defined before you begin to enter calculable data.

do it !

Enter the documentation and row labels for a spreadsheet.

1. On Sheet1 of a blank workbook, click cell A2 to make it the active cell.

2. Type Income and Expenses for Best Tech Stores, and then click the Enter button ☑ to the right of the Name box to confirm the entry. The label will appear in the Formula bar as you type. Even though the label is longer than the the cell's width, it will be displayed in its entirety because the cell to the right of it is empty. Your screen should look like Figure 1-12.

3. Click cell A4 and type the label Pathname:. Then press [Tab] and type f:\backup\spreadsheet\Quarterly Income Report.xls in cell B4. This is a fictional file path meant to represent that which might be used for a workbook stored on a network server. The path will not change throughout this book even though the file names you use will.

4. Click cell A5 and type Author:. Then press [Tab] and type: Kyle Samuel in cell B5.

5. Click cell A6 and type Ranges:. Press [Enter] on the keyboard to confirm the entry and move the cell pointer to cell A7.

6. Enter Date: in cell A7 and April 26, 2002 in cell B7. Then click cell A8. Notice that Excel changes the date you entered to a short format. Enter Assumption: Sales Growth in cell A8, press [Tab], and then enter .1 in cell B8. Press [Enter]. Notice that the label in cell A8 is cut off because cell B8 is not empty.

7. Press [Enter] two times to make cell A11 the active cell. Then type Income, press [Enter], and type Sales in cell A12.

8. Press [Enter] twice and make the following entries: A14—Expenditures, A15—Rent, A16—Salaries, A17—Miscellaneous, A18—Total Expenses, A20—Gross Profit. Press [Enter] after the last entry. Your worksheet should look like Figure 1-13. ◖◗ If your screen resolution is not set to at least 800 by 600 pixels, you likely will have to scroll down in order to complete the above entries.

9. Leave this worksheet on your screen as you will need it in the next Skill.

more

The Enter button on the Formula bar confirms cell entries just like pressing the [Enter] key on the keyboard does, except using the Enter button leaves the cell pointer in the current cell instead of moving it to the cell below. The Enter button disappears after you use it, but you can bring it back by clicking the text box in the Formula bar. The Cancel button ☒ next to the Enter button removes the contents from the active cell and restores the cell's previous contents, if there were any.

Excel automatically assumes that a number is a value and aligns it to the right by default. If you wish to use a number as a label, simply type an apostrophe ['] before the number. Excel will then align the data to the left as a label. The apostrophe will be hidden in the cell, but will appear in the Formula bar.

If you start to enter a label whose first few letters match those of an adjacent cell in the column, Excel's AutoComplete feature will complete the label to match the other one. If you do not wish to accept the suggestion, simply continue typing to overwrite the suggestion.

Figure 1-12 Entering a label

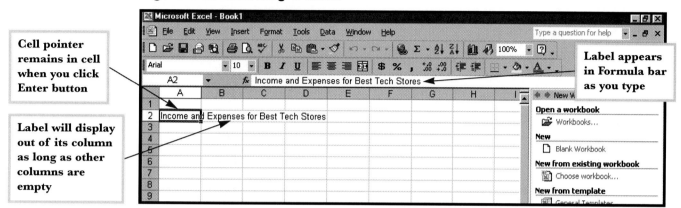

Cell pointer remains in cell when you click Enter button

Label appears in Formula bar as you type

Label will display out of its column as long as other columns are empty

Figure 1-13 Worksheet with labels added

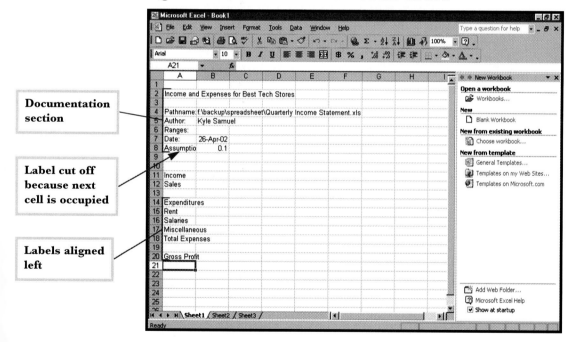

Documentation section

Label cut off because next cell is occupied

Labels aligned left

Practice

Click the New button ⬜ on the Standard toolbar to open a new workbook (the Task Pane may disappear). Beginning in cell A2, enter the following cell labels, pressing [Enter] after each: your name, today's date, your instructor's name, the title of the course you are taking, and Practice1-5. Leave this file open and go on to the next Skill.

skill

Saving and Closing a Workbook

concept

Saving your work is essential to being an effective computer user. By saving your files with unique names on storage devices such as hard drives, floppy disks, network drives, or Web servers, you can return to your workbooks after you have exited Excel. You also should save changes made to files frequently while you are still working on them. Saving frequently minimizes the amount of data you would lose in the event of a system crash or power failure. Closing a document removes it from the screen and puts it away for later use. You can close a file while leaving the application open in order to work with other Excel files. Or, if you are finished using Excel, you can exit the application.

do it !

Save a workbook in a folder you create specifically for your Excel files.

1. You should have two Excel files open from the previous Skill—one from the do it! section and one from the Practice section. Click Window on the Menu bar, and then click the name of the file from the do it! section—most likely named Book1. Book1 will now be the active file.

2. Click File, then click Save As to open the Save As dialog box, shown in Figure 1-14. (If you had chosen the Save command instead of Save As, the Save As dialog box would have appeared anyway, as this is the first time you are saving this file.) The file name Book1.xls automatically appears selected in the File name text box, ready to be changed. A menu command that is followed by an ellipsis (three dots) indicates that a dialog box accompanies the command. Dialog boxes permit you to set options before executing a command.

3. To give the workbook file a more distinctive name, type Quarterly Income Statement.xls. The default name, Book1.xls, will be overwritten. Windows 95 and newer versions of Windows support file names of up to 255 characters. The file name may contain uppercase or lowercase letters, numbers, and many, but not all, symbols.

4. Excel's default storage location is your computer's My Documents folder, so that folder name appears selected near the top of the dialog box in the Save in drop-down list box. To select a different location, click the Save in box to open its drop-down list, or click one of the buttons on the Places bar on the left side of the dialog box. If you have been instructed to save your Student Files on a floppy disk, open the Save in drop-down list now and click 3½ Floppy (A:) to select your floppy disk drive. Otherwise, leave the Save in box set to My Documents (or follow the specific directions of your instructor).

5. Click the Create New Folder button to the right of the Save in box. The New Folder dialog box, shown in Figure 1-15, will appear.

(continued on EX 1.18)

Figure 1-14 Save As dialog box

Places bar: click a button to select a common storage location quickly

Your Contents window may show different files and folders

Click to open Web browser to a search page

Click to change view of items in Contents window

Click to move up one level in your file hierarchy

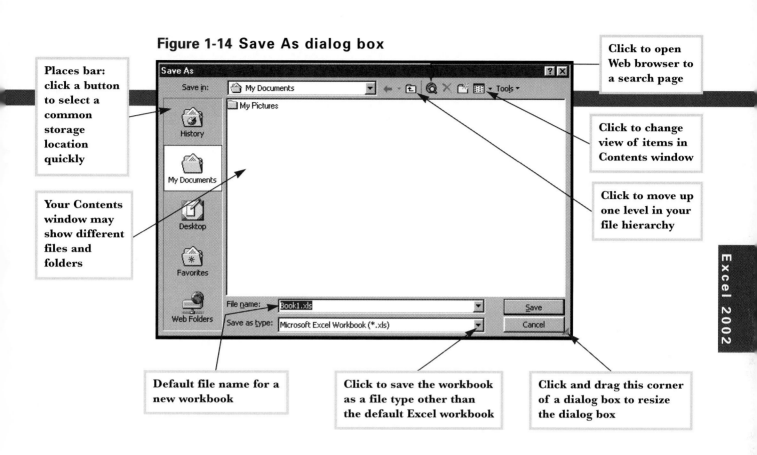

Default file name for a new workbook

Click to save the workbook as a file type other than the default Excel workbook

Click and drag this corner of a dialog box to resize the dialog box

Figure 1-15 New Folder dialog box

Type name of new folder here

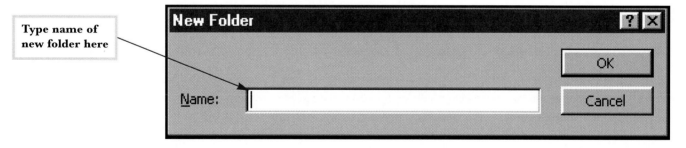

skill Saving and Closing a Workbook (continued)

do it!

6. Since an insertion point already appears in the Name text box, you can begin entering a name for the new folder. Type Excel Files as the name of the new folder.

7. Click the OK button ⬚ OK ⬚ in the New Folder dialog box to create the new folder. The New Folder dialog box closes returning you to the Save As dialog box. The new folder you just created for your Excel files is selected in the Save in box (see Figure 1-16). The folder you just created is a subfolder of the My Documents folder (or the location you selected in step 4) because that folder was selected in the Save in box when you clicked the Create New Folder button.

8. Click the Save button ⬚ Save ⬚ in the bottom-right corner of the Save As dialog box to save the Quarterly Income statement workbook in your newly created Excel Files folder. Notice that when the dialog box closes, the new file name appears in the application window's Title bar.

9. Click File, then click Close. Excel removes Quarterly Income Statement.xls from the worksheet window. The workbook you created for the Practice exercise in the previous Skill should remain open.

more

Understanding the difference between the Save command and the Save As command is an important part of working with productivity software like Excel. When you save a new file for the first time, the two commands function identically: they both open the Save As dialog box, allowing you to choose a name, storage location, and file type for the file. Once you have saved a file, the commands serve different purposes. Choosing the Save command, or clicking the Save button 🖫 on the Standard toolbar, will update the original file with any changes you have made, maintaining the same file name, storage location, and file type. The previous version of the file will no longer exist. Choosing the Save As command will permit you to save a different version of the same file, with a new name, location, type, or any combination of the three.

Another safeguard against losing data is Excel's AutoRecover feature. AutoRecover creates a "recovery" file that stores your most recent changes every time the feature activates. If your system crashes or you lose power before you have a chance to save your work, the recovery file will open the next time you start Excel. The recovery file will contain all changes you made through the last AutoRecover before the interruption. To control the AutoRecover settings, click Tools on the Menu bar, and then click the Options command. In the Options dialog box, click the Save tab, which is shown in Figure 1-17. From the Save tab, you can control whether AutoRecover is used at all, how frequently the feature runs, and where the recovery file is stored on your computer. You also may disable AutoRecover in the active workbook while leaving it available to all other workbooks. Keep in mind that using AutoRecover is not a replacement for saving your files—it is merely a backup plan. Running Auto-Recover every ten minutes is an effective amount of time because it is frequent without interfering. If you run AutoRecover too often, you could save unwanted changes. In addition, older computers may experience a slow-down for a few seconds while AutoRecover runs.

Figure 1-16 Saving a file in a new folder

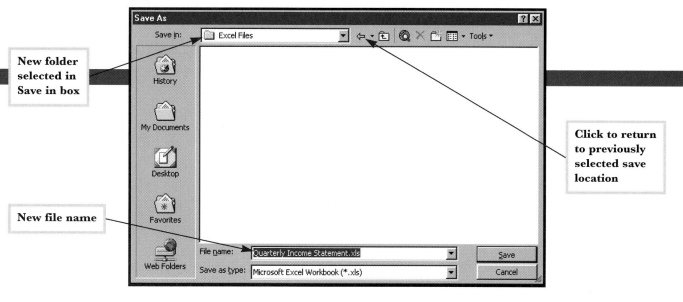

New folder selected in Save in box

Click to return to previously selected save location

New file name

Figure 1-17 Save tab of Options dialog box

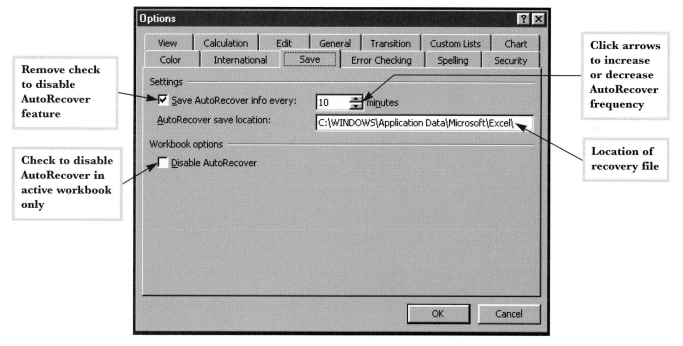

Remove check to disable AutoRecover feature

Check to disable AutoRecover in active workbook only

Click arrows to increase or decrease AutoRecover frequency

Location of recovery file

Practice

Save the workbook you created in the Practice exercise for the previous Skill in your Excel Files folder using the file name myexprac1-6.xls. Then close the file.

skill Opening a Workbook

concept

To view or edit a worksheet that has been saved and closed previously, you must open the workbook file from the location in which it was stored. Since Excel spreadsheets are associated with the Excel application by the .xls file extension in their file names, you can double-click an Excel file in My Computer or Windows Explorer and Excel will launch automatically. However, if you are already working in Excel, you can open Excel files from directly within the application. If the Student Files for this book have been distributed to you on a floppy disk or CD-ROM, make sure you have inserted the disk in the proper drive for this Skill.

do it !

Open an existing Excel workbook that was saved previously.

1. With the Excel application running, click the Open button 📂 on the Standard toolbar. The Open dialog box will appear. You will recognize many features of the Open dialog box from the Save As dialog box. You also can access the Open dialog box by clicking File on the Menu bar and then clicking the Open command on the File menu.

2. Click the box labeled Look in near the top of the dialog box to open a list of the locations available to your computer (see Figure 1-18).

3. Click 3½ Floppy (A:) on the list if your Student Files are stored on a floppy disk. If your Student Files are stored on a local or network drive, ask your instructor for the name of the drive you should select.

4. If your Student Files are stored in a folder on your floppy disk or hard disk, you will need to double-click that folder in the Contents window of the dialog box. Otherwise, you already should see a list of files in the Contents window. Click the file named exdoit1-7.xls to select it. It is possible that your computer is set to hide file extensions of known file types, in which case you should click exdoit1-7.

5. Click the Open button [Open ▾] in the bottom-right corner of the dialog box. The workbook file you selected appears in the Excel window.

6. Click the Close button [X] on the right end of the Menu bar to close the file.

more

If you cannot remember the name or location of the file you wish to open, Excel provides a search tool to help you. To access this help, click the Tools button [Tools ▾] in the Open dialog box, and then click the Search command on the Tools menu (see Figure 1-19). The Search dialog box, shown in Figure 1-20, will open. On the Basic tab of the Search dialog box, you can search for files that contain specific text that you know to be in the file you need to find. You can also choose which locations the search will cover, such as all of My Computer or just the (C:) drive, and what file types the search will include. The Advanced tab allows you to search using numerous other criteria including the date when a file was last modified, the name of the person who created it, or a portion of the file name.

Excel can open a variety of file types. If you know you have selected the correct drive or folder but you still do not see your file listed in the Contents window, make sure that the Files of type box displays a setting that includes Excel files.

If you click the arrow on the right edge of the Open button, you can open the selected document in a specific manner. If you select Open Read-Only, Excel will not allow any changes to be saved unless you use Save As to create a new file. Open as Copy creates a new copy of the file so you can keep the old version and edit the new one. Open in Browser becomes active when you have selected an HTML document. The selected file will open in your default Web browser instead of Excel. Open and Repair assists you in opening and recovering a document that has been damaged by a program, system, or power failure.

Figure 1-18 Selecting a Look in location in the Open dialog box

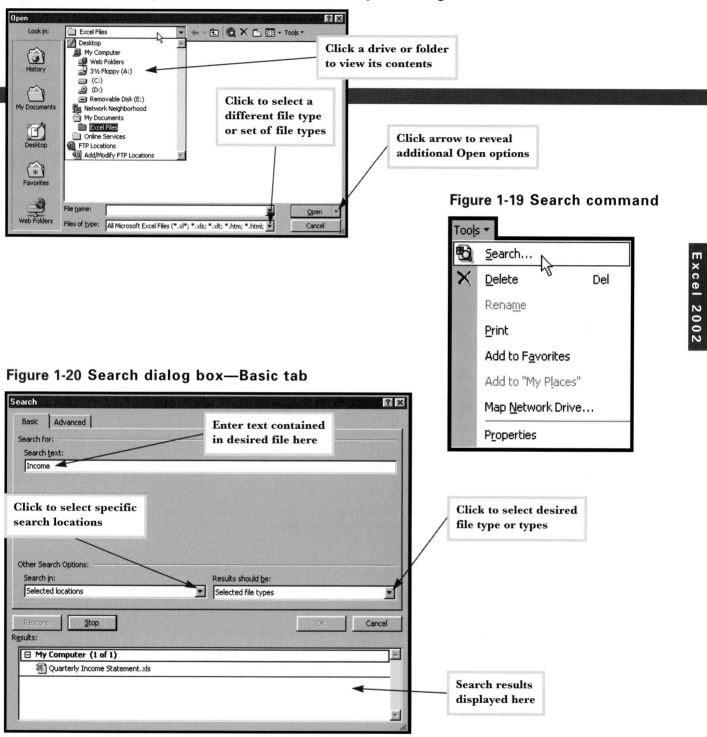

Figure 1-19 Search command

Figure 1-20 Search dialog box—Basic tab

Practice

To practice opening a workbook, open the Student File named exprac1-7.xls. Use the Save As command to save this file in your Excel Files folder with the file name myexprac1-7.xls. Close the file and leave Excel running when you are done.

skill

Editing a Cell's Information

MOUS *Skill*

concept

Many spreadsheets are used over a long period of time and receive constant updates. For example, suppose you work in the billing department of a company that supplies oil to homes for heating purposes. You might use a spreadsheet that tracks how much oil each customer takes upon each delivery. In order to calculate how much to bill the customers, you would also need to enter the price of oil, which changes frequently. Instead of starting a new worksheet each time the price changes, you simply can update the figure on the same worksheet. Editing the contents of a cell is very similar to editing text in a word processing document.

do it !

Edit the contents of one cell in the Formula bar and another in the cell itself.

1. Open the Student File exdoit1-8.xls.

2. Click cell A14. The cell pointer moves to cell A14 and Expenditures is displayed in the Formula bar.

3. Move the mouse pointer over the Formula bar, position it between the n and the d in the word Expenditures (the mouse pointer should appear as I-beam I when over the Formula bar), and click. A blinking insertion point will appear, the Formula bar buttons will display, and the mode indicator on the Status bar will read Edit, as shown in Figure 1-21.

4. Press and hold the left mouse button, and then drag the I-beam to the right over the last seven letters of the word Expenditures. That portion of the cell entry is now selected.

5. Type ses to replace the selected text. The cell entry now reads Expenses instead of Expenditures (see Figure 1-22).

6. Click cell B5 to make it the active cell.

7. Type your own name. As soon as you begin typing, Excel deletes the current contents of the cell, the name Kyle Samuel.

8. Click the Cancel button ☒ on the Formula bar. Excel deletes your name from cell B5 and restores the cell's previous entry.

9. Save this file in your Excel Files folder using the file name QIS-Editing.xls, and then close the file.

more

As you saw in the exercise above, when you click a cell and immediately begin typing, Excel deletes the existing cell contents immediately. To edit the contents of a cell within the cell, instead of in the Formula bar, without deleting the cell's existing contents, double-click the cell. A blinking insertion point will appear in the cell where you double-clicked, allowing you to edit the cell contents in the same way as you would in the Formula bar. You can press the [Backspace] key on the keyboard to remove characters to the left of the insertion point, or press the [Delete] key to remove characters to the right of the insertion point. You also can press the left and right arrow keys on the keyboard to move the insertion point in the cell without deleting any characters. Once you are in Edit mode in a cell, double-clicking in the cell a second time will select all of the cell's contents. ⬛ If you make a mistake while working in Excel, you can reverse your last action by clicking the Undo button 🔄▾ on the Standard toolbar. Click the arrow next to the Undo button to open a list of all your previous actions in the current work session, permitting you to undo multiple actions at once. Your most recent action will be at the top of the list. If you undo an action other than the most recent, all actions that followed the one you select will be undone as well. The Redo button 🔁 enables you to reverse the effect of the Undo button.

Figure 1-21 Editing a cell in the Formula bar

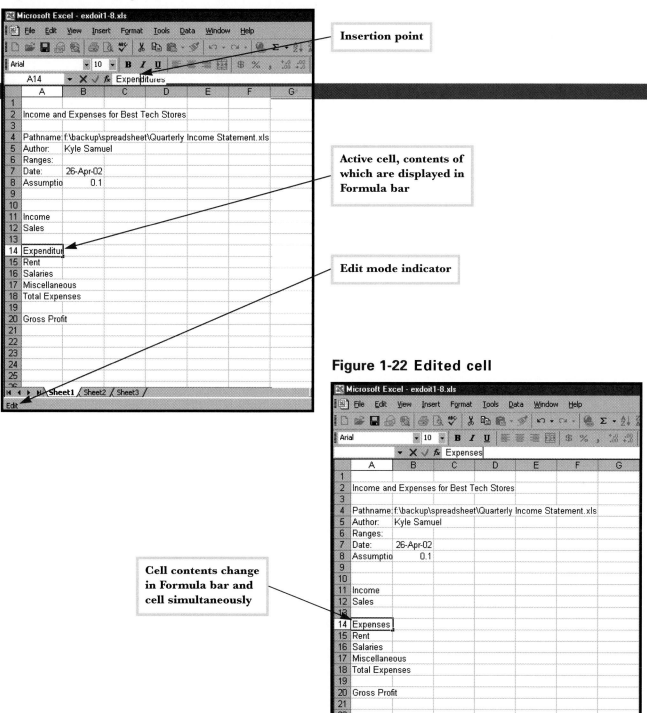

Figure 1-22 Edited cell

Excel 2002

Practice

To practice editing information in a cell, open the Student File exprac1-8.xls and save it in your Excel Files folder as myexprac1-8.xls. Then change the first initial and last name (R. Patel) in cell A1 to your own first initial and last name using the Formula bar. Change the name (Raj Patel) in cell B4 to your name working within the cell itself. When you are done, click the Save button [💾] on the Standard toolbar to save the changes you have made to the worksheet, and then close the file.

skill | Using the Office Assistant

concept

Even experienced computer users occasionally need help using software correctly. Excel offers a number of built-in help features that you can use when you encounter problems or when you simply have a question about a particular aspect of the program. One of these features is the Office Assistant, an animated character who provides several kinds of help. When turned on, the Assistant will provide tips related to your current activity. The Assistant also will sense when you are trying to complete a specific task and offer to guide you through it. Or you can ask the Assistant a question.

do it !

Ask the Office Assistant about Task Panes.

1. Click Help on the Menu bar, then click Show the Office Assistant. The Office Assistant will appear on your screen.

2. Click the Office Assistant to open its dialog balloon, and then type What's the difference between a workbook and a worksheet? as shown in Figure 1-23.

3. Click the Search button `Search`. The Assistant searches Excel's Help files for answers to your question and then presents a list of suggested topics.

4. Click the topic named About viewing workbooks and worksheets, as shown in Figure 1-24. A Help window containing the topic you selected appears alongside the Excel window (see Figure 1-25).

5. Read the Help file, and then click its Close button ⊠ to remove it from the screen. Notice that the Ask a Question drop-down list box `What's the difference betw ▾` on the right end of the Menu bar now contains the question you asked the Office Assistant. This gives you quick access to the Help topic in case you want to consult it again.

6. Click Help on the Menu bar, then click Hide the Office Assistant. The Assistant removes itself from the screen.

more

Each question you ask the Office Assistant during an Excel session is added to the Ask a Question drop-down list. To access the questions you have asked previously, click the arrow at the right end of the Ask a Question drop-down list box. When you click a question on this list, the list of suggested Help topics found earlier by the Office Assistant will appear. You then can click the topic of your choice. If you want to ask a new question without using the Office Assistant, click inside the Ask a Question box itself, type your new question, and press [Enter] on the keyboard. The Ask a Question drop-down list is erased when you exit Excel.

When the Office Assistant is showing and has a tip for you, a lightbulb icon 💡 will appear above the Assistant. Click the lightbulb to receive the tip.

Once you have hidden the Assistant several times, you will be asked if you would prefer to turn off the feature instead of just hiding it. The option of turning off the Assistant is also available in the Options dialog box, which you can access by clicking the Options button `Options` in the Assistant's dialog balloon. The Options tab in the Office Assistant dialog box, shown in Figure 1-26, also allows you to control how the Assistant behaves and what kinds of help it provides. The Gallery tab contains animated characters that you may use as your Office Assistant in place of the default paper clip character. While previews of the other Office Assistant characters are available on the Gallery tab, you must install the characters from your Excel 2002 or Office XP CD-ROM in order to use them.

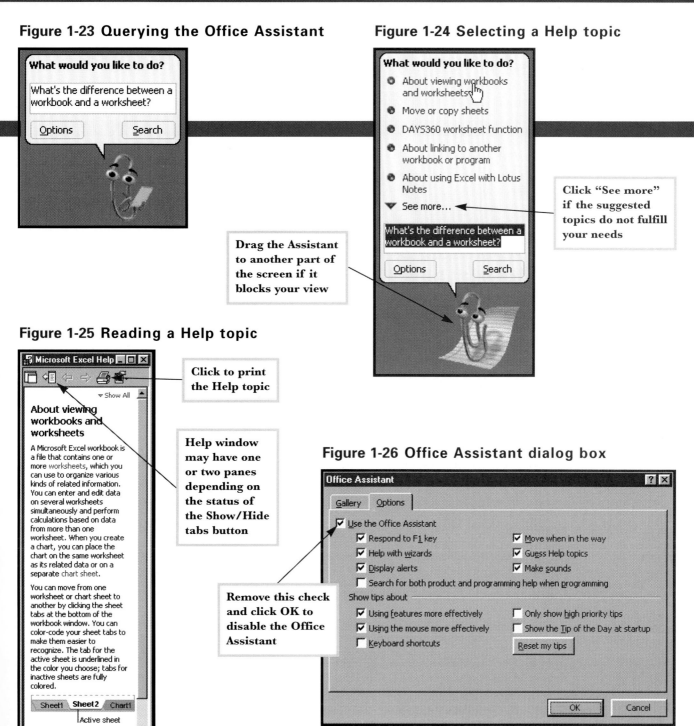

Figure 1-23 Querying the Office Assistant

Figure 1-24 Selecting a Help topic

Drag the Assistant
to another part of
the screen if it
blocks your view

Click "See more"
if the suggested
topics do not fulfill
your needs

Figure 1-25 Reading a Help topic

Click to print
the Help topic

Help window
may have one
or two panes
depending on
the status of
the Show/Hide
tabs button

Figure 1-26 Office Assistant dialog box

Remove this check
and click OK to
disable the Office
Assistant

Practice

Use the Office Assistant to read Help files on the following topics: new features in Excel, ScreenTips, and Smart Tags. If you have a printer available, print any one of the Help files that you view. Close the Help window, and then turn off the Office Assistant as described in the More section and as depicted in Figure 1-26 above.

skill Other Excel Help Features

concept

For those that would prefer to obtain help without making use of the Office Assistant, Excel offers a number of alternatives. As you have seen, ScreenTips help you identify elements of the Excel window such as toolbar buttons. The What's This? command expands the power of ScreenTips to include feature names and descriptions of their functions. Perhaps most important of all, all of Excel's Help files are available to you in an extensive Microsoft Excel Help facility that operates independently of the Office Assistant. If you have not turned off the Office Assistant as instructed on the previous page, do so now.

do it !

Use the What's This? command and the Help facility to improve your knowledge of Excel.

1. Click ☐ to open a blank workbook. Then open the Help menu from the Menu bar and click the What's This? command. The mouse pointer now appears with a question mark attached to it.

2. Click ✓ on the Standard toolbar with the What's This? pointer. A ScreenTip appears with an explanation of the item you clicked (see Figure 1-27).

3. Click the mouse again to erase the ScreenTip.

4. Click the Microsoft Excel Help ② button on the Standard toolbar. The Microsoft Excel Help window opens alongside the application window with links to particular areas of help and a list of commonly requested help topics.

5. Click the Show button ⬚ at the top of the Help window. The window expands so that you can see the Help tabs. The Answer Wizard tab functions just like the Office Assistant, allowing you to ask a question and receive a list of suggested Help topics. ◕ If you see the Hide button ⬚ instead of the Show button, you do not need to complete this step.

6. Click the Index tab, which allows you to search an alphabetical list of keywords.

7. Begin to type filetype in the text box labeled 1. Type keywords. Before you finish typing, the scrolling list box below will have scrolled to match what you typed.

8. Click the Search button [Search] to find Help topics related to the selected keyword. The found topics will be listed in the box labeled 3. Choose a topic (see Figure 1-28). The first topic will be selected and the text of its related Help file will appear in the right pane of the Help window. Read the text of this Help file, scrolling down as necessary.

9. Click the Help topic titled Change the program that starts when you open a file. Read the text of this Help file and then click one of the subtopic links below the text to read more (see Figure 1-29).

10. Click the Close button ☒ in the Help window to close Microsoft Excel Help.

more

The Contents tab in the Microsoft Excel Help window is organized like an outline or the table of contents you might find in a book. It begins with a main level of broad topics symbolized by book icons, each of which can be expanded to reveal more specific subtopics. You can click these subtopics on the Contents tab to display their related Help files on the right side of the window, just as on the Index tab. In addition to the Show/Hide toggle button, the Help toolbar has buttons for organizing the application and Help window (Auto Tile), browsing through the Help topics you have viewed (Back and Forward), printing a topic, and opening a menu of Options.

Figure 1-27 What's This? ScreenTip

Spelling (Tools menu)

Checks spelling in the active document, file, workbook, or item.

Click to begin new keyword search

Figure 1-28 Help topics found by keyword

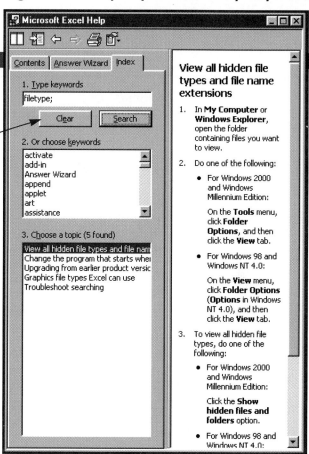

Figure 1-29 Viewing a subtopic

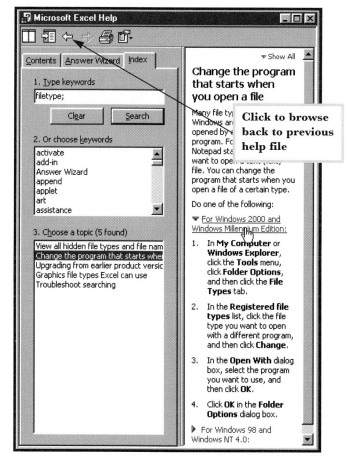

Practice

Open the Microsoft Excel Help facility and use the Index tab to find Help topics related to the keyword keyboard. Then read the Help file for the topic titled Keyboard shortcuts. Also read the subtopic in that file titled Display and use the Help window. Close the Help window when you are done. Finally, use the What's This? command to get help on the Standard toolbar's Search button. When you have completed this Practice exercise, close all open workbooks.

shortcuts

Function	Button/Mouse	Menu	Keyboard
Create a new workbook	▯	Click File, then click New	[Ctrl]+[N]
Open a workbook	📂	Click File, then click Open	[Ctrl]+[O]
Confirm a cell entry	✓		[Enter], [Tab], or arrow keys
Cancel a cell entry	✕	Click Edit, then click Undo Typing	[Ctrl]+[Z]
Save a workbook for the first time	💾	Click File, then click Save or Save As	[Ctrl]+[S]
Save changes to existing workbook	💾	Click File, then click Save	[Ctrl]+[S]
Save workbook with new name, location, file type		Click File, then click Save As	[Alt]+[F], [A]
Close the active workbook	✕	Click File, then click Close	[Ctrl]+[W]
Close the application	✕	Click File, then click Exit	[Alt]+[F4]
Undo last action	↺	Click Edit, then click Undo [action]	[Ctrl]+[Z]
Redo last undone action	↻	Click Edit, then click Redo [action]	[Ctrl]+[Y]
Get Help	❓	Click Help, then click Show the Office Assistant or Microsoft Excel Help	[F1]
Search for a file from Open dialog box	Tools ▾ Then click Search		
Search for a file from Task Pane in application window	🔍	Click File, then click Search	[Alt]+[F], [H]

A. Identify Key Features

Name the items indicated by callouts in Figure 1-30.

Figure 1-30 Elements of an Excel spreadsheet

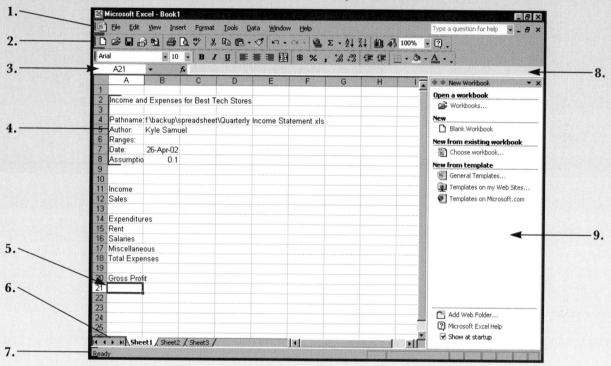

1.
2.
3.
4.
5.
6.
7.
8.
9.

Excel 2002

B. Select the Best Answer

10.	Click this to make the Excel window fill the screen	a.	Name box
11.	Displays the active cell address	b.	Save command
12.	Gives you feedback on your current activity in Excel	c.	Cell
13.	Enables you to choose a name and location for storing a file	d.	Maximize button
14.	Saves the changes you have made to your file keeping its name and location	e.	Label
15.	Unit created by the intersection of a row and a column	f.	Status bar
16.	A location where you can edit the contents of a cell	g.	Save As command
17.	Text in a cell that describes data displayed on the worksheet	h.	Formula bar

quiz (continued)

C. Complete the Statement

18. To select an entire column, click:

a. The first cell in the column

b. Any cell in the column

c. Its letter column heading button

d. The corresponding row number

19. Pressing [Ctrl]+[Home] will:

a. Move your view up one screen

b. Move your view down one screen

c. Move the cell pointer to cell A1

d. Move the cell pointer to column A in the current row

20. All of the following actions will move the cell pointer to another cell except:

a. Clicking the Enter button

b. Pressing the Enter key

c. Pressing the Tab key

d. Pressing an arrow key

21. A well-designed spreadsheet does not necessarily require:

a. Documentation

b. Multiple worksheets

c. Input

d. Output

22. All of these are Excel help features except:

a. The Index tab

b. The Office Assistant

c. What's This?

d. The Help Wizard

23. A file extension:

a. Allows you to see a hidden file

b. Lets you edit the information in a cell

c. Associates a file with a specific application

d. Is a component of Excel's Help facility

24. A workbook can contain up to:

a. 16 worksheets

b. 255 worksheets

c. 3 worksheets

d. 65,536 worksheets

25. Excel assumes that numbers entered on a worksheet are:

a. Values

b. Labels

c. Formulas

d. Apostrophes

26. The cell whose address is B5 is located in:

a. Row B, column 5

b. Row B, cell 5

c. Column B, row 5

d. The Name box

27. To view Sheet tabs that are not visible in the window:

a. Go to another worksheet

b. Open a new workbook

c. Use the horizontal scroll bar

d. Use the Sheet tab scrolling buttons

interactivity

Build Your Skills

1. Open the Excel application and document a new spreadsheet:

   a. Use the Start button to start Microsoft Excel.

   b. Add a documentation section to the blank worksheet using the title Class Schedule, your name, and the date.

   c. When you document the file name, use the name extest1.xls.

   d. Include labels for Ranges and Macros. Your documentation section should occupy rows 1–6 of the worksheet.

2. Design a worksheet that displays your daily class schedule:

   a. Add labels in row 8 for the days of the week, not including Saturday and Sunday. Start in cell B8 and skip a column between each day. Friday should be in cell J8.

   b. Add labels in column A for your class periods. Enter the time of your earliest class period in cell A10, and then add a label for each subsequent class period through your last class of the day. Skip a row between each time label.

   c. Enter the names of your classes in the appropriate cells where the day of the week and the time intersect.

3. Get help using the Office Assistant and the Help tabs:

   a. Use the Help menu to show the Office Assistant.

   b. Open the Office Assistant's dialog balloon.

   c. Ask the Assistant for information on how to customize toolbars.

   d. Select the Help topic titled About toolbars and read its associated Help file.

   e. Use the Index tab in the Microsoft Excel Help window to search for Help topics related to the keyword install.

   f. Select and read the Help topic titled What's installed with Excel.

   g. Close the Help window and turn off the Office Assistant from the Options tab of the Office Assistant dialog box.

4. Save a workbook file and exit Excel:

   a. Save the workbook you were constructing in steps 1 and 2 in your Excel Files folder using the file name extest1.xls.

   b. Use the File menu to exit Microsoft Excel.

interactivity (continued)

Problem Solving Exercises

1. Create a new spreadsheet following the design principles you learned in Lesson 1. Design this spreadsheet to log your daily activities. Enter labels for the days of the week just as you did in the previous exercise, but this time add Saturday and Sunday after Friday and do not leave a blank column between each day. Instead of class periods, add labels down column A for Class, Activities, Meals, Studying/Homework, Leisure, and Sleep. Do not skip rows between labels. Save the file in your Excel Files folder as 7-Day Daily.xls.

2. Due to a recent merger, your accounting firm can now increase the budgets of several departments. You are pleased to learn that you will have an additional $10,000 available for your expense account. As a member of the Human Resources department, you know how much this money will help you in your efforts to attract the top candidates for your company's job openings. Use Excel to design a spreadsheet that will detail your strategy for utilizing the new funds over the next year. You do not have to enter any monetary values yet. Simpy set up the structure of the worksheet with documentation and labels. One set of labels should divide the year in periods, such as months or quarters, and the other set should specify specific uses of the new funds, such as recruiting trips, additional job postings, or presentation materials. Save the spreadsheet in your Excel Files folder as New HR Funds.xls.

3. The restaurant you manage has been using an old computer running primitive software for its day-to-day operations. You have finally convinced the owner of the restaurant to invest in a new computer and the Office XP software suite. Now you have to prove that the purchase was a wise investment. Using Excel, design a spreadsheet that will allow you to keep track of the waitstaff's schedule over one week. Your worksheet should include columns for Time in and Time out each day of the week. Save the file in your Excel Files folder as Staff Schedule.xls.

4. Create the worksheet shown in Figure 1-31 to the best of your ability.

Figure 1-31 Lab Inventory.xls

	A	B	C	D	E	F	G	H	I	J	K	L
1	Lab Inventory											
2	Pathname:	C:\Department\Reports\Lab Inventory.xls										
3	Author:	Montgomery Moncrief										
4	Ranges:	Equipment										
5	Date:	2/3/02										
6												
7	Equipment		# Remaining		# Needed		Cost per unit		Cost to department			
8	250ml beaker											
9	400ml beaker											
10	250ml Erlenmeyer flask											
11	200ml Florence flask											
12	10ml graduated cylinder											
13	100ml graduated cylinder											
14												
15												
16												
17												
18												
19												
20												
21												
22												
23												
24												
25												

Sheet1 / Sheet2 / Sheet3 /

When you are done, replace the name in cell B2 with your own name and save the file in your Excel files folder as Lab Inventory.xls.

Manipulating Data in a Worksheet

One of the greatest advantages of using spreadsheet software is that it automates many of the processes that take up so much time when done by hand. In Excel you can enter data quickly and easily, then move or copy data from one location to another just as quickly and easily.

Excel also automates your calculations by using mathematical formulas. If you instruct Excel what operation to perform, and where to get the data, the program will execute the calculations for you. The Paste Function feature prevents you from having to enter complicated formulas that Excel already knows. Once you have entered a formula or a function, you can even paste it to a new location.

Often, businesses like to use the data they have gathered to make projections about their business. In Excel you can use assumed values, or assumptions, to perform calculations under different conditions, altering the results of the worksheet each time. This technique is called What-If Analysis, and takes full advantage of Excel's versatility.

Lesson Goal:

Fill out a worksheet with values, then use Excel's Cut, Copy, and Paste features to manipulate the labels and values in the worksheet. Use the newly located values to perform calculations with the help of formulas and functions. Change the output of the worksheet by performing a What-If Analysis. Finally, print a copy of the worksheet.

skills

- ≩ Cutting, Copying, and Pasting Labels
- ≩ Entering Values
- ≩ Entering Formulas
- ≩ Using Functions
- ≩ Using the Insert Function Feature
- ≩ Copying and Pasting Formulas
- ≩ Using What-If Analysis
- ≩ Previewing and Printing a Worksheet

skill
Cutting, Copying, and Pasting Labels

concept

Excel makes it easy to transfer text from cell to cell. Cutting or copying information places it on the Office Clipboard. The Office Clipboard enables you to temporarily store text, data, and/or graphics from any Office XP program (and many other programs) and then paste them into any other Office XP program. In Office XP, the Clipboard can hold up to 24 items. (If you copy a 25th item, the Clipboard deletes the first one.) If you exit all Office programs, or click Clear All on the Office Clipboard, all Clipboard items are deleted. Clicking the Paste command inserts at the insertion point the last item that you sent to the Clipboard. You also can move cell contents by clicking the border of a cell or group of cells, then dragging and dropping them at a new location.

do it !

Enter sales and expense values in an income statement worksheet.

1. Open Student File exdoit2-1.xls and save it as QIS-Cutting.xls.

2. Click cell C6, click Edit, and click Cut. A moving border will appear around cell C6, indicating that you now can remove its contents (see Figure 2-1). Click cell A7, click Edit, and click Paste. The contents of cell C6 will move to cell A7.

3. Right-click cell E6 to display a shortcut menu, click Cut, right-click cell A8 to open another shortcut menu, and click Paste. The contents of cell E6 will move to cell A8. Excel (and the other Office programs) often allow you to right-click an area to display a shortcut menu with commands related to that area. For many Office commands, using a shortcut menu avoids having to move the mouse pointer to a toolbar to find a command.

4. Click cell B10, and type the text Q1, standing for Quarter 1 of what will be an income statement for four quarters of a year. Click the Enter button ☑ between the Name box and Formula bar to confirm the entry (see Figure 2-2). The insertion point will disappear.

5. With cell B10 still selected, click Edit, then click Copy. (As with the Cut command, the Copy command will produce a moving border around the selected cell.) Select cells C10 through E10 (see Figure 2-3). Press [Enter]. The contents of cell B10 now appear in the three additional cells, and the moving border around cell B10 disappears.

6. Click cell C10. Click in the Formula bar right after the numeral 1, press [Backspace], press [2], and press [Tab] to move to cell D10. Click in the Formula bar right after the numeral 1, press [Backspace], press [3], and press [Tab] to move to cell E10. Click in the Formula bar right after the numeral 1, press [Backspace], press [4], and click cell B12. Cells B10 to E10 now read Q1, Q2, Q3, and Q4 to represent the four financial quarters of the calendar year.

7. Save the changes you have made to the worksheet and close the file.

more

To move the contents of a cell or cell group to another location, you also can click the left mouse button on the gray border of the area you wish to move to display the mouse pointer with a four-way arrow [⇱]. Drag the border of the selected area to the new location. As you drag, a lighter gray border matching the size of the area being dragged will move with the mouse pointer. When the lighter gray border rests over the desired location, release the mouse button. The cell contents then will appear in the destination cell with the darker border around it.

To copy the contents of a cell or cell group rather than just move them, hold down [Ctrl] while clicking the left mouse button, drag the cell border, and then release it at the new location. When you copy cell contents, a mouse pointer and small cross ( ) will tell you that you are copying rather than moving the contents.

Steps 5 and 6 show you how to copy cell contents and then increase a numbered sequence with the Formula bar. However, you can create a numbered sequence more quickly by using Excel's AutoFill feature. To use AutoFill, click the lower-right corner—or fill handle—of the first cell in your sequence. While holding down the mouse button, drag the fill handle to the right or down, depending on the desired direction, and release the mouse pointer when you reach the last cell in the row or column to which you want to copy the source cell's contents. For a detailed explanation of using AutoFill, see the Skill entitled "Filling a Cell Range with Labels" in Lesson 3.

The Concept section of this Skill states that clicking the Paste command inserts at the insertion point the last item that you sent to the Clipboard. However, to paste a different item, click the destination cell, click Edit, click Office Clipboard to display the Clipboard task pane, and click the item on the task pane that you want to paste. To paste all items at once, display the Clipboard, then click the Paste All button at the top left of the task pane.

Figure 2-1 Copying a cell

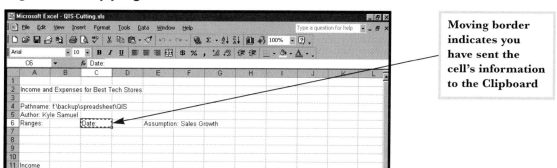

Moving border indicates you have sent the cell's information to the Clipboard

Figure 2-2 Enter button

Enter button appears when you enter text or data in cell but have not yet confirmed it

Figure 2-3 Selected destination cells

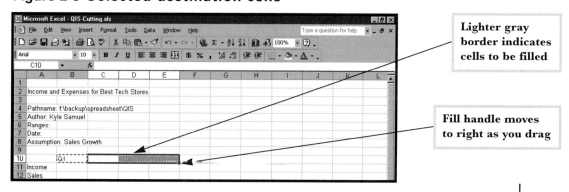

Lighter gray border indicates cells to be filled

Fill handle moves to right as you drag

Practice

To practice cutting, copying, and pasting labels, follow the instructions on the Practice2-1 Sheet tab of the practice file exprac2.xls. Save changes as myexprac2-1.xls and close the file. Make sure you have the More section of this Skill before starting the Practice exercise. Also, please see the note on Smart Tags toward the bottom of the Practice2-1 worksheet.

skill

Entering Values

concept

Values are numbers, dates, or times that Excel uses in calculations. They are the main reason that Excel exists—so that you can easily and quickly enter, manipulate, and permanently record numerical data. When entering and confirming the data, you do so in the same way as you do with labels.

do it !

Enter Sales and Expenses values in a worksheet.

1. Open Student File exdoit2-2.xls and save it as QIS-Entering.xls.

2. Click cell B12 to make it the active cell. Type 168500, then press [Tab]. The first quarter sales now appears in the cell, and the cell pointer moves to the right to cell C12. Enter the rest of the Sales values in the same row, pressing [Tab] after each: 179000, 190000, and 210000. ◖◗ Some Excel users will want to add commas to separate the thousands place from the hundreds, but should avoid doing so. Information on using comma separators appears in Lesson 3. Also, when typing numbers, make sure you use only digits and not letters such as O instead of 0 (zero). One way to avoid making this mistake is to use the numeric keypad on the right side of the keyboard when entering numbers. If your numeric keypad does not seem to be working, press the Num Lock key.

3. Click cell B15 to activate it. Type 20000 as the first quarter's rent expense and click ☑. Using the Edit command, copy this value to cell C15 (see Figure 2-4). Click in cell D15, and type an increased rent expense of 21000. Click ☑. Right-click in the cell and, using the shortcut menu, copy this value to cell E15 (see Figure 2-5).

4. Click cell B16 to activate it. Enter the following four values into the Salaries row, pressing [Tab] after entering each value except the last: 95000, 97500, 105000, and 108500.

5. Click cell B17 to activate it. Enter the following four values into the Miscellaneous row, pressing [Tab] after entering each value including the last: 13500, 14500, 16500, and 19000. ◖◗ In Step 4, you did not need to press [Tab] after the last value because clicking in cell B17 confirmed the entry in cell E16. However, you did need to press [Tab] after cell E17 because there are no more entries to be made in this Skill. You also could have pressed [Enter] or clicked ☑ to confirm the last entry.

6. Verify that your values match those in Figure 2-6. Re-enter any numbers that do not match the figure, save the changes you have made to the worksheet, and close the file.

more

You may have noticed that when you entered the values they aligned to the right when confirmed, not to the left like the text labels. Excel aligns values to the right by default and recognizes an entry as a value when it is a number or is preceded by +, −, =, @, #, or $. Excel recognizes ordinals (1st, 2nd, 3rd, etc.) and other combinations of numbers and letters as labels rather than values.

Sometimes you may want to use a number, such as a year, as a label. In such cases, you must type an apostrophe (') before the number so Excel will recognize that number as a label and will disregard it when performing calculations. The apostrophe will not appear in the cell, but will appear in the Formula bar above the worksheet window when you select the appropriate cell.

Figure 2-4 Edit command

Figure 2-5 Shortcut menu

Editing commands appear on left, with matching Shortcut key combinations on right

Icons in gray area corresponds with buttons on tool-bars

Shortcut menus often display commands found on tool-bar menus

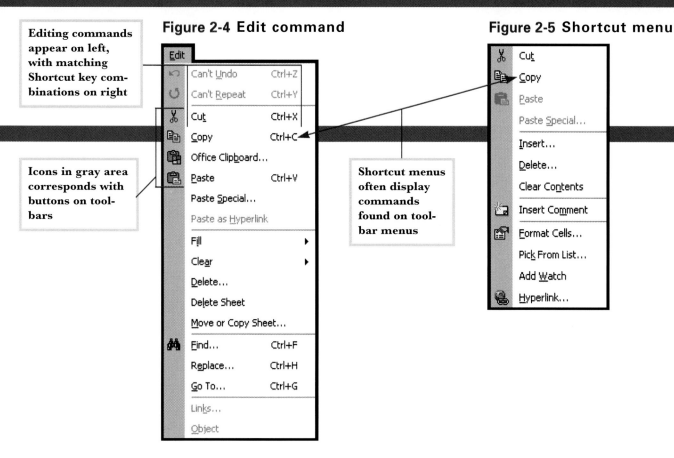

Figure 2-6 Worksheet's appearance after entering values

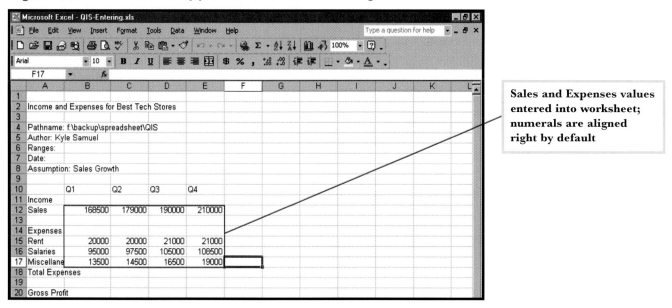

Sales and Expenses values entered into worksheet; numerals are aligned right by default

Practice

To practice entering values, follow the instructions on the Practice2-2 Sheet tab of practice file exprac2.xls. Save changes as myexprac2-2.xls and close the file.

Excel 2002

skill | Entering Formulas

concept

Formulas are mathematical equations that perform calculations such as averages, sums, or products on worksheet data. An Excel formula always starts with an equal sign (=) to distinguish the formula from text or data. Typical Excel formulas contain cell references, mathematical operators (the symbols dictating the kind of calculation to perform), and—quite often—numerical values. For example, in the formula =B5+2, the combination B5 is a cell reference, the plus sign (+) is an operator, and the number 2 is a value. By using formulas instead of filling in averages, totals, and so on by hand, your worksheet saves you the trouble of inputting new results each time a value changes. Also, as long as your formulas are correct and relevant to the values you calculate, any changes in values automatically will produce correct results.

do it !

Calculate the Total Expenses and Gross Profit for each quarter of the income statement.

1. Open Student File exdoit2-3.xls and save it as QIS-Formulas.xls.

2. Click cell B18 to activate it. Enter the formula =B15+B16+B17 to add the three types of expenses (you can type a lowercase b). As you type the cell references, colored rectangles will appear around them, matching the references in the formula. (see Figure 2-7).

3. Click the Enter button ☑. The calculated result 128500 will appear in cell B18 as the total of the three cells referenced in the formula. The formula itself will appear in the Formula bar. Notice that the part of the words Total Expenses in cell A18 that ran into cell B18 is covered when you type the formula. Information on widening columns to display all text in a cell appears in Lesson 3.

4. Click cell C18, and enter the formula =C15+C16+C17 to add the three types of expenses in column C. In cells D18 and E18, repeat Steps 2 and 3, substituting the letters D and E respectively in each of the three cell references, and pressing [Tab] after each formula.

5. Click cell B20, enter the formula =B12-B18, and press [Tab]. Excel will subtract the first quarter's Total Expenses from the first quarter's Sales to arrive at the result 40000 for the first quarter's Gross Profit.

6. Repeat Step 4 to enter similar formulas into cells C20, D20, and E20, However, substitute the letters C, D, and E respectively where you used the letter B for the two cell references, and press [Tab] after each formula.

7. Verify that your worksheet matches Figure 2-8. If necessary, correct any incorrect formulas to ensure the same calculated results. If you are absolutely sure that all of your formulas are correct, double-check the values that you are referencing.

8. Save the changes you have made to the worksheet and close the file.

more

As this Skill demonstrates, Excel formulas use cell addresses and the arithmetic operators + for addition and – for subtraction. However, the standard computer keyboard does not contain the traditional multiplication and division symbols. Therefore, computer keyboards use the asterisk (*) for multiplication and the forward slash (/) for division. The carat mark (^) expresses exponentiation (raising a number to another power). If you select two or more cells containing values, their sum will appear in the Status bar below the horizontal scroll bar. If you right-click the sum in the status bar, a shortcut menu will display so you can select other forms of calculation.

Figure 2-7 Entering a formula

Formula from selected cell displays in Formula bar

Color of referenced cell matches color in formula

Formula in cell B18 partially covers text in cell A18

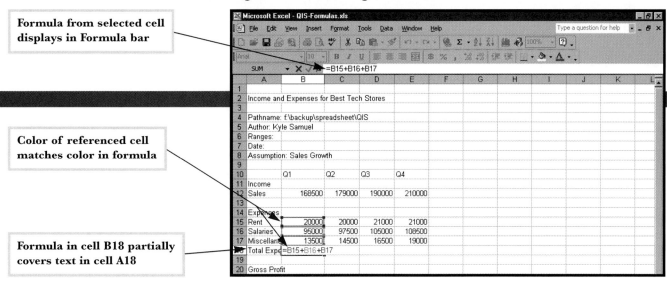

Figure 2-8 Calculating Total Expenses and Gross Profit

Calculated results appear in cells containing formulas

Calculated results in cell B20 also partially obscure text in cell A20

Formula does not display in Formula bar when cell pointer sits over empty cell

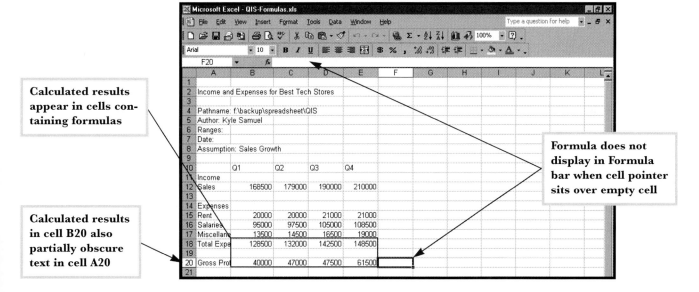

Practice

To practice entering formulas, follow the instructions on the Practice2-3 Sheet tab of the practice file exprac2.xls. Save changes as myexprac2-3.xls and close the file.

skill | Using Functions

concept

You can, of course, type a new formula each time that you want to perform a calculation in a worksheet. However, using predefined formulas, called functions, can reduce the time and trouble of typing out formulas. Excel has hundreds of these built-in formulas, and they cover the most common types of calculations you might use in a worksheet, such as AVERAGE, SUM, RATE, and so on.

do it !

Use the SUM function instead of typing in a formula to calculate Total Expenses.

1. Open Student File exdoit2-4.xls and save it as QIS-Functions.xls.

2. Click cell B18 to activate it. Click the AutoSum button ⎡Σ⎤⎡▾⎤ (not on down-arrow to its right). The AutoSum function automatically enters the formula to add the values of the cells directly above the active cell. The SUM formula =SUM(B15:B17) appears in cell B18 and the Formula bar. The cells being added (called the function argument) are surrounded by a moving border. Below the active cell a ScreenTip appears showing the syntax (or structure) of the formula, including the form of the argument (see Figure 2-9). The argument contains the notation B15:B17, or a cell range, referring to all cells between and including B15 and B17. More information on cell ranges appears in Lesson 3.

3. Press the AutoSum button again to confirm Excel's calculation and to apply the formula to the active cell. The value 128500, matching the value that appeared before using AutoSum, appears in the cell, verifying that the AutoSum function has included the proper cells in the total. ⬤ Instead of clicking the AutoSum button again, you could press [Enter] or [Tab].

4. Click cell F10 to activate it, and type a new label, Yearly Total. Click cell F12, then click the AutoSum button ⎡Σ⎤⎡▾⎤. This time, a moving border appears around the cells directly to the left of cell F12. In F12 itself, the SUM function appears, followed by the correct cell range, B12:E12. The formula also appears in the Formula bar, and a ScreenTip appears, displaying a generic example of the formula (see Figure 2-10).

5. Click AutoSum again to confirm Excel's calculation and to apply the formula. The value 747500 will appear in the cell (see Figure 2-11).

6. Save the changes you have made to the worksheet and close the file.

more

In this Skill you used the AutoSum button to enter the SUM function into cell B18 in place of the formula =B15+B16+B17. However, unlike AutoSum, most Excel functions require users to enter additional information manually after the function name. This information, enclosed, or "nested," in parentheses and called the argument, can be cell references or other data that the function needs to calculate a result. The function acts upon the argument, as the SUM function acted upon the range of cells enclosed in the parentheses that followed the function.

Sometimes the cells you want to reference in an AutoSum do not appear directly above the active cell. In such cases, click the cell where you want the calculated result to appear, click the AutoSum button, click and drag through the cells desired for the argument, and press [Enter] or [Tab].

Figure 2-9 Using AutoSum to add cells in a column

Moving border indicates argument of formula

AutoSum formula with cell references "nested" in parentheses

ScreenTip displays syntax, or structure, and arguments of selected function

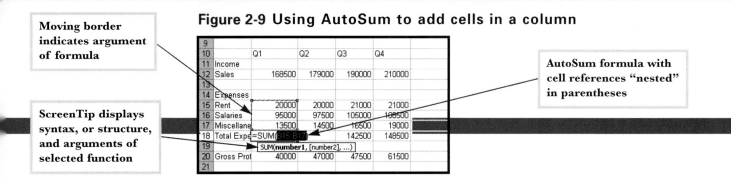

Figure 2-10 Using AutoSum to add cells in a row

Moving border

ScreenTip

AutoSum formula

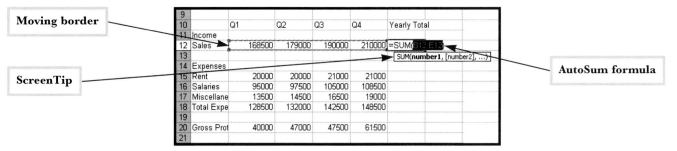

Figure 2-11 Worksheet's appearance after using AutoSum twice

Click AutoSum button once to display formula; click again to apply formula

SUM formula displays in Formula bar

Type new label in cell F10

Yearly Total of Sales in cell F12 results from using AutoSum function

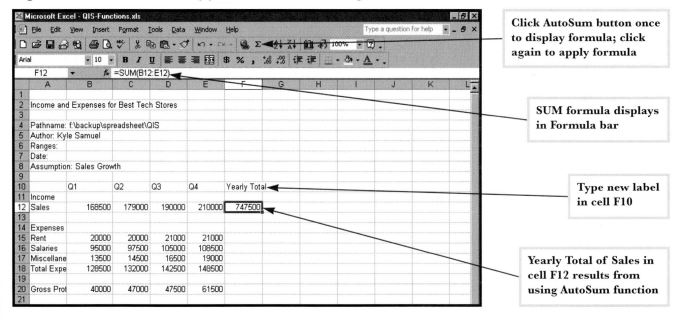

Practice

To practice entering functions, follow the instructions on the Practice2-4 Sheet tab of practice file exprac2.xls. Save changes as myexprac2-4.xls and close the file.

skill | Using the Insert Function Feature

concept

To enter a function other than SUM, you can either enter it yourself or use the Paste Function command. This command enables you to insert built-in formulas into your worksheet, saving you the trouble of remembering mathematical expressions and the time it takes to type them. And to help you find just the right function for a desired calculation, Excel 2002 has a sophisticated Insert Function dialog box that provides even more help than did earlier versions of the dialog box.

do it !

Use the Paste Function command and the Insert Function dialog box to calculate the average Total Expenses for the year.

1. Open Student File exdoit2-5.xls and save it as QIS-Insert Function.xls. Click cell A22, enter the abbreviation Avg. Exp. (Average Expenses), and press [Tab] to move to cell B22.

2. With cell B22 selected, click Insert, then click Function. The Insert Function dialog box will open, with the Search for a function text box highlighted by default. Type the description Calculate average of quarterly expenses, then click the Go button. In the Or select a category list box, the word Recommended will appear. In the Select a function list box, a list of functions will appear that Excel estimates will satisfy your calculation needs.

3. In the Select a function list box, click the AVERAGE function. The function name, the form of the related argument, and a description of what the function does will appear in the gray area directly below the list box (see Figure 2-12).

4. Click [OK]. The Insert Function dialog box will close, and the Function Arguments dialog box will open with the cell range B20:B21 appearing by default in the Number1 text box. However, this is not the cell range you want to average. If necessary, drag the dialog box out of the way so it does not block your view of row 18.

5. With the Number1 text box still highlighted, click cell B18, drag into cell E18, and release the mouse button. As you drag, a moving border will appear around the selected cells, and the Function Arguments dialog box will collapse to a smaller size. When you release the mouse button, the dialog box will re-expand, and the formula =AVERAGE (B18:E18) will appear in cell B22 and in the Formula bar (see Figure 2-13).

6. Click [OK] to apply the formula and to close the dialog box. The calculated result 137875 will display in cell B22, representing the quarterly average of Total Expenses (see Figure 2-14). Save the changes you have made to the worksheet and close the file.

more

When you open the Insert Function dialog box, the default setting for the Or select a category list box is Most Recently Used. At the same time, the Select a function list box lists the functions you have used most often in the recent past. If you have not used the Insert Function command before, the Most Recently Used category will contain a default list of commonly used functions. Each most recently used function also appears under the other general categories listed in the Or select a category list box. To find functions other than most recent ones, click the desired general category in the Or select a category list box. A list of specific functions within the general category will appear in the Select a function list box. Scroll up and down in that list box to find and click on the desired function.

Notice that the Number1 option in the Function Arguments dialog box is bold. This indicates that you must enter data into that text box in order for the function to work. Plain text in the dialog box indicates that entering cell ranges there is optional.

Figure 2-12 Insert Function dialog box

Type brief description of desired calculation, then click [Go] to display list of functions that might perform that calculation

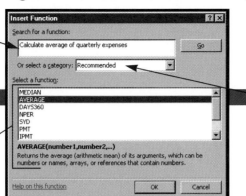

Select function category from drop-down list of related functions; select "All" category if desired function does not appear in specific category

Click specific function to display function name, form of related argument, and brief description of what function does

Figure 2-13 Selecting an argument for a function

Cell range of selected argument

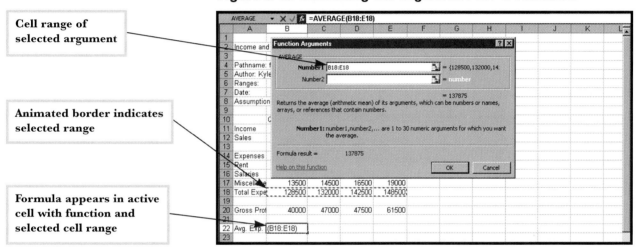

Animated border indicates selected range

Formula appears in active cell with function and selected cell range

Figure 2-14 Inserted AVERAGE function

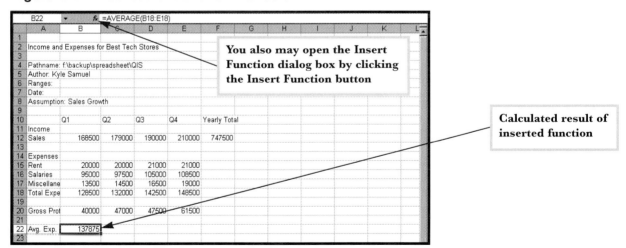

You also may open the Insert Function dialog box by clicking the Insert Function button

Calculated result of inserted function

Practice

To practice inserting functions, follow the instructions on the Practice2-5 Sheet tab of the practice file exprac2.xls. Save changes as myexprac2-5.xls and close the file.

skill | Copying and Pasting Formulas

concept

You can copy and paste formulas into other cells just as you can with labels and values. By default, Excel considers the cell referred to in an argument as a relative cell reference. A relative cell reference (such as A1, B5, H16, and so on) is based on the relative position of the cell with the formula and the cell referred to by the reference. If the position of the cell with the formula changes, the cell reference changes too. With relative cell references, in other words, formulas in new locations automatically adjust to reference new cells.

do it !

Copy the SUM function from cell F12 into cells F13 through F20 to calculate Yearly Totals for Expenses and Gross Profit. Delete unneeded formulas in cells referring to empty cells to the left.

1. Open Student File exdoit2-6.xls and save it as QIS-Copying.xls.

2. Click cell F12 to activate it. Although the Yearly Total for Sales appears in the cell, the SUM function appears in the Formula bar with the argument B12:E12 inside parentheses.

3. Click the Copy button 📋 to copy the formula to the Office Clipboard. An animated border will appear around cell F12.

4. Click cell F15 to activate it. Click the Paste button 📋▾, not the down-arrow to its right, to paste the copied function into cell F15. The result 82000 will appear in cell F15. Notice that Excel has changed the argument in the Formula bar from B12:E12 to B15:E15, which is the cell range relative to the copied function's new position in the worksheet (see Figure 2-15). With this new argument the function will be applied to the row in which it appears rather than the one it was copied from.

5. A Paste Options Smart Tag appears at the lower right of cell F15. Move the mouse pointer over the Smart Tag, and click the down-pointing arrow to display a shortcut menu with the default option Keep Source Formatting (see Figure 2-16). Since this is the desired option, leave the Tag as is.

6. Move the mouse pointer over the lower-right corner of cell F15 (the cell's fill handle). The pointer will change to a black cross (✚). Holding down the mouse button, drag into cell F20 to copy the function from cell F15 into the newly selected cells as well. A gray border will appear around the cell range as you drag, and an Auto Fill Options Smart Tag will appear at the lower right of cell F20 . Release the mouse button at the lower-right corner of cell F20 (see Figure 2-17).

(continued on EX 2.14)

Figure 2-15 Copying and pasting a function

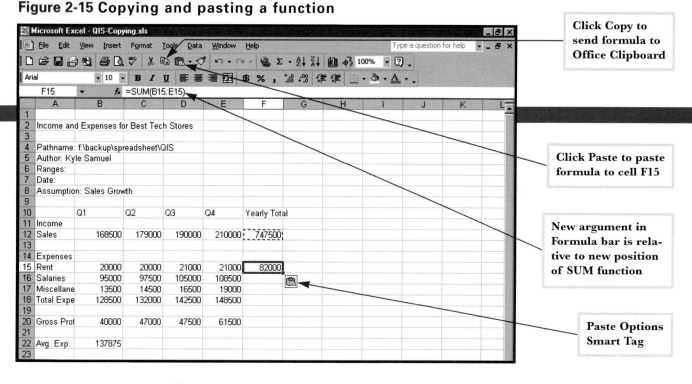

Click Copy to send formula to Office Clipboard

Click Paste to paste formula to cell F15

New argument in Formula bar is relative to new position of SUM function

Paste Options Smart Tag

Figure 2-16 Paste Options Smart Tag

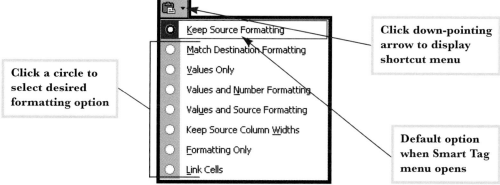

Click down-pointing arrow to display shortcut menu

Click a circle to select desired formatting option

Default option when Smart Tag menu opens

Figure 2-17 Using the fill handle to copy a function

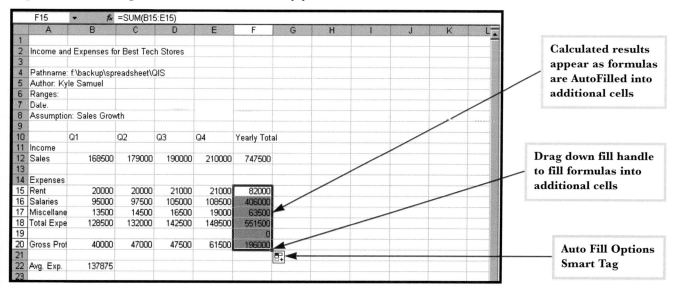

Calculated results appear as formulas are AutoFilled into additional cells

Drag down fill handle to fill formulas into additional cells

Auto Fill Options Smart Tag

skill | Copying and Pasting Formulas (cont'd)

do it !

7. Move the mouse pointer over the Smart Tag at the lower right of cell F20. Click the down-pointing arrow to display a shortcut menu with the default option Copy Cells (see Figure 2-18). Since this is the desired option, leave the Tag as is.

8. Cell F19 contains a zero because the function copied into that cell adds up the empty cells directly to the left of the cell. Since you do not need a function in cell F19, click in that cell and press [Delete]. Click cell F22.

9. Verify that the cell values in your worksheet match those in Figure 2-19. If any cells do not match, double-check the formulas in the mismatched cells and correct them. If you are absolutely sure that all your formulas are correct, double-check the values of the cells that are referenced by the newly pasted formulas.

10. Save the changes you have made to the worksheet and close the file.

more

As the Concept section of this Skill mentions, a relative cell reference is based on the relative position of the cell with the formula and the cell referred to by the reference. Relative cell references appear quite often in formulas. Relative cell references contrast with absolute cell references, which you can identify by the dollar signs that precede their column letters and row numbers (such as $A$1, $B$5, $H$16, and so on). In a formula an absolute cell reference always refers to one cell in a specific, unchanging location. Therefore, if the position of the cell with a formula changes, the absolute cell reference in that formula will not change, but stay the same. With absolute cell references, in other words, formulas in new locations do not adjust to reference new cells. While this Skill took advantage of the flexibility of relative cell references, the next Skill will take advantage of the benefits of absolute cell references.

Figure 2-18 Auto Fill Options Smart Tag

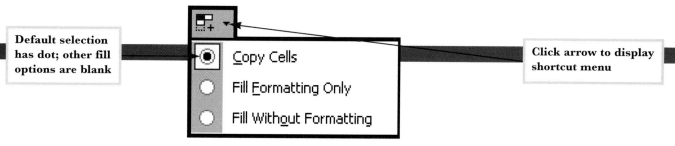

Default selection has dot; other fill options are blank

Click arrow to display shortcut menu

Figure 2-19 Worksheet's appearance after deleting unneeded function

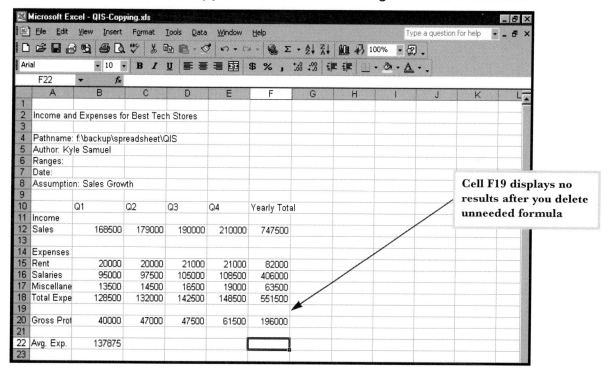

Cell F19 displays no results after you delete unneeded formula

Practice

To practice copying and pasting formulas, follow the instructions on the Practice2-6 Sheet tab of practice file exprac2.xls. Save changes as myexprac2-6.xls and close the file.

skill Using What-If Analysis

concept

Excel facilitates changing the conditions in one area of a worksheet to see how such changes will affect calculations in another area. This altering of conditions is called What-If Analysis, and is one of Excel's most useful and time-saving features in personal and in business worksheets. Imagine, for example, that you wanted to buy a new car but could not figure out by how much a larger down payment would reduce monthly payments. A properly designed worksheet would be able to calculate such a figure. Likewise, an income statement like Best Tech's could use What-If analysis to estimate increasing Sales and how they would affect Gross Profits.

do it !

Determine how Sales would grow and how Gross Profits would be affected, assuming a Sales Growth assumption of 10% per quarter.

1. Open Student File exdoit2-7.xls and save it as QIS-Analysis.xls.

2. Select cells C12, D12, and E12—that is, the sales figures for the second, third, and fourth quarters of the year. Press [Delete] to remove the values from the selected cells. The values in cells C12:E12 now are considered to be zero. Notice that the values in cells F12 and C20:F20 change. This change results from the fact that Excel automatically recalculates formulas when values in their referenced cells have been changed.

3. Click cell C8 to activate it. Enter .1 (10% expressed as a decimal) into the active cell. This is the cell that will be referenced in the formula that calculates projected earnings. Press [Enter]. Notice that Excel inserts a zero before the .1 in cell C8 as a place holder (see Figure 2-20).

4. Click cell C12 to activate it. Here, you must create a formula to multiply the first quarter's sales by 110%, which will show the result in the second quarter of a 10% increase over the first quarter's sales figure. Enter the formula =B12*(1+$C$8) into the active cell (see Figure 2-21). The dollar signs preceding the column letter C and the row number 8 tell Excel not to change the cell address, even if you move the formula to a new location. This unchanging cell address is an absolute cell reference. To create an absolute cell reference, be sure to place a $ before both the column letter and row number. If you place a $ before only the column letter or the row number, only the part of the formula with the symbol will remain absolute, while the other part will remain relative.

5. Press [Enter]. The result of the calculation, 185350, appears in place of the formula in cell C12. Cells F12 and C20 change to reflect Excel's recalculation of their formulas, which include cell C12 in their arguments.

6. Click cell C12 again, and move the mouse pointer over the cell's fill handle. While holding down the mouse button, drag into cell E12 to copy the formula in cell C12 to the two additional cells. As you drag, a gray border appears around cells C12:E12, and shading appears in cells D12 and E12 to indicate that you have used the fill handle to copy the formula in C12 into the shaded cells.

(continued on EX 2.18)

Figure 2-20 Cell values deleted and sales growth assumption added

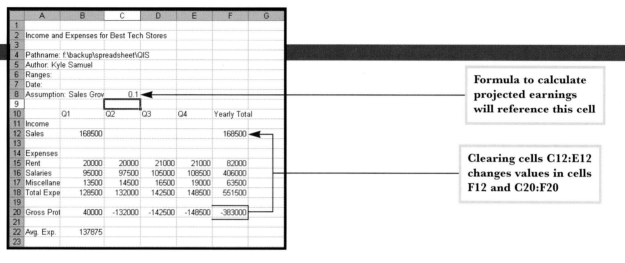

	A	B	C	D	E	F	G
1							
2	Income and Expenses for Best Tech Stores						
3							
4	Pathname: f:\backup\spreadsheet\QIS						
5	Author: Kyle Samuel						
6	Ranges:						
7	Date:						
8	Assumption: Sales Grov		0.1				
9							
10		Q1	Q2	Q3	Q4	Yearly Total	
11	Income						
12	Sales	168500				168500	
13							
14	Expenses						
15	Rent	20000	20000	21000	21000	82000	
16	Salaries	95000	97500	105000	108500	406000	
17	Miscellane	13500	14500	16500	19000	63500	
18	Total Expe	128500	132000	142500	148500	551500	
19							
20	Gross Prof	40000	-132000	-142500	-148500	-383000	
21							
22	Avg. Exp.	137875					
23							

Formula to calculate projected earnings will reference this cell

Clearing cells C12:E12 changes values in cells F12 and C20:F20

Figure 2-21 Growth assumption formula using absolute cell reference

SUM   X ✓ ƒx   =B12*(1+$C$8)

	A	B	C	D	E	F	G	H	I	J	K	L
1												
2	Income and Expenses for Best Tech Stores											
3												
4	Pathname: f:\backup\spreadsheet\QIS											
5	Author: Kyle Samuel											
6	Ranges:											
7	Date:											
8	Assumption: Sales Grov		0.1									
9												
10		Q1	Q2	Q3	Q4	Yearly Total						
11	Income											
12	Sales	168500	=B12*(1+$C$8)			337001.1						
13												
14	Expenses											
15	Rent	20000	20000	21000	21000	82000						
16	Salaries	95000	97500	105000	108500	406000						
17	Miscellane	13500	14500	16500	19000	63500						
18	Total Expe	128500	132000	142500	148500	551500						
19												
20	Gross Prof	40000	36501.1	-142500	-148500	-214499						
21												
22	Avg. Exp.	137875										
23												

Cell B12 is relative cell address, while cell C8 is absolute cell address

skill

Using What-If Analysis (cont'd)

do it !

7. Notice that the Auto Fill Options Smart Tag appears to the lower right of cell E12. Since the default option in the Smart Tag is the desired one, click cell F13 and press [Delete] to hide the Smart Tag.

8. Click cell D12. Notice that the cell's reference to cell B12 has changed to C12, but that the reference to cell C8 remains the same (see Figure 2-22). If you had not included the dollar signs before the column letter and row number, the copied formula would have replaced the cell reference C8 with D8, an empty cell, and the result in D12 would have been wrong. Click cell A1 (see Figure 2-23).

9. Save the changes you have made to the worksheet and close the file.

more

Formulas can contain several operations. An operation is a single mathematical step in solving an equation, such as adding two numbers, multiplying a cell by a percentage, or calculating an exponent—that is, raising a number to another power. When working with formulas containing multiple operators, Excel performs the calculations in the order displayed in Table 2-1 below. For example, in the formula =6+3*4, Excel would multiply 3 by 4 to get 12, then add 6 to get 18. However, if you want to change the order of calculations, you must add parentheses around the part of the formula that you want to calculate first. For example, in the formula =(6+3)*4, Excel would add 6 and 3 to get 9, then multiply 9 by 4 to get 36.

In a more complicated formula, such as =(B5+10)/SUM(C5:E5), Excel first would add the value in cell B5 and the quantity of 10, then divide the result by the total of the values in the cell range C5:E5. Because Excel allows you to use many operators and worksheets can have many cells, you must know how to reference cells correctly and construct formulas properly. You then must be willing to double-check the effectiveness of your formulas before saving them in a finalized worksheet and, especially, handing them off to another person to use with reliability.

Table 2-1 Order of Operations

Operator	Description
–	Negation, as in –10
%	Percentage
^	Exponentiation
* and /	Multiplication and division, from left to right
+ and –	Addition and subtraction, from left to right
&	Connection of two strings of text (concatenation)
=, <, >, <=, >=, and <>	Comparisons

Figure 2-22 Formula containing relative and absolute cell references

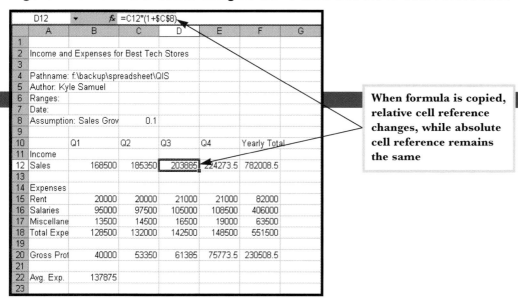

When formula is copied, relative cell reference changes, while absolute cell reference remains the same

Figure 2-23 Sales growth assumptions added to Quarters 2 through 4

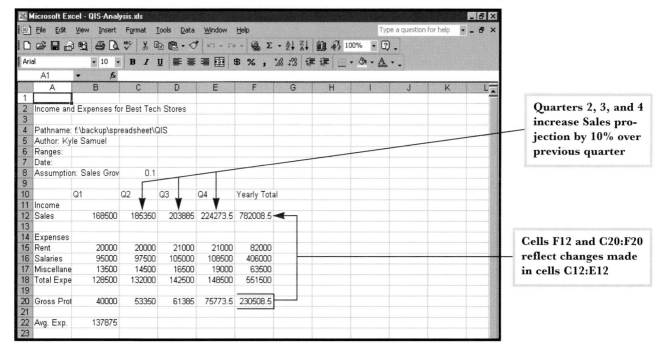

Quarters 2, 3, and 4 increase Sales projection by 10% over previous quarter

Cells F12 and C20:F20 reflect changes made in cells C12:E12

Practice

To practice performing a What-If Analysis, follow the instructions on the Practice2-7 Sheet tab of practice file exprac2.xls. Save changes as myexprac2-7.xls and close the file.

skill

Previewing and Printing a Worksheet

 MOUS skill

concept

Printing a worksheet is useful if you need a paper copy to refer to, to distribute to others, or to file. While offices are becoming more and more electronic, many people still prefer working with paper documents over viewing them on a screen. Excel allows you to view a worksheet as it will appear on a printed page before it is printed so you can spot errors or items you would like to change before going through the printing process.

do it!

Display a worksheet in Print Preview mode, then print it.

1. Open Student File exdoit2-8.xls and save it as QIS-Previewing.xls. Replace the author's name in cell A5 with your own name.

2. Make sure your computer is properly connected to a working printer, that the printer is turned on and loaded with paper, and so on (if necessary, ask your instructor for help).

3. Click the Print Preview button 🔍 on the Standard toolbar. The worksheet will display in Print Preview mode, and the mouse pointer will appear as a magnifying glass (see Figure 2-24).

4. Click near the top of the preview page. The worksheet will be magnified so you can examine it more closely, and the pointer will change to an arrow. By default, worksheet gridlines are non-printing items, so they will not appear in the preview.

5. On the Print Preview toolbar, click the Print button Print... . The view will revert to regular mode and the Print dialog box will open (see Figure 2-25). If you do not need to conduct a print preview or adjust the settings in the Print dialog box, you can print the active worksheet by clicking the Print button 🖨 on the Standard toolbar.

6. Click OK . The Print dialog box will close, a box will appear notifying you of the print job's progress, and the document will be sent to the printer.

7. Verify that the printer has printed your document. If it has not, do **not** reprint. Instead, check the connection between your computer and the printer, the condition of the printer itself, and so on. Reprint the document only after you have found the printing problem. Again, if needed, ask your instructor for help.

8. Close your worksheet without saving any changes to the file.

more

You can adjust many printing options by selecting the Page Setup command on the File menu. The Page Setup dialog box will open with four tabs: Page, Margins, Header/Footer, and Sheet. The Page tab controls the way the printed selection will appear on a page, such as its vertical (Portrait) or horizontal (Landscape) orientation, or by how large or small you can scale it on one or more pages. The Margins tab controls how you adjust the amount of space between a worksheet's print area and the edges of a page. The Header/Footer tab controls what information will appear at the top and/or bottom of each page of a printout, such as page numbers, titles, file names, author's name, and so on. The Sheet tab controls how you present your data on the printed page, such as whether to print gridlines, which parts of the worksheet to print, and whether to repeat column headings across each new page.

Figure 2-24 Previewing your worksheet

Click here to open Print dialog box

Click with magnifier to zoom in on document

Click "Close" button to return to Normal view

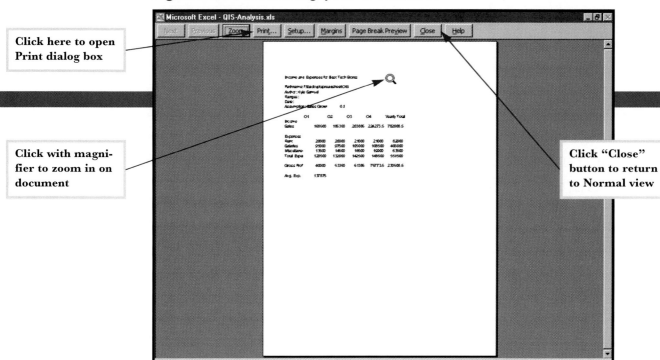

Figure 2-25 Print dialog box

Name of selected printer

Click "All" to print all pages of a multi-page document, or enter page numbers to print a partial range of pages

Opens printer-specific dialog box to adjust settings for paper, graphics, and other printer features

Specifies that all of the current worksheet will print

Alternate way to access Print Preview mode

Click arrows or enter a number to change quantity of copies to print

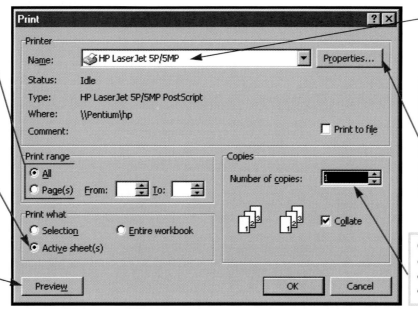

Practice

To practice previewing and printing a worksheet, follow the instructions on the Practice2-8 Sheet tab of practice file exprac2.xls. Save changes as myexprac2-8.xls and close the file.

shortcuts

Function	Button/Mouse	Menu	Keyboard
Cut data to the Clipboard	✂	Click Edit, click Cut	[Ctrl]+[X]
Copy data to the Clipboard	📋	Click Edit, click Copy	[Ctrl]+[C]
Paste data from the Clipboard	📋 ▾	Click Edit, click Paste	[Ctrl]+[V]
AutoSum	Σ ▾		
Insert Function	ƒx	Click Insert, click Function	
Print Preview	🔍	Click File, click Print Preview	
Print	🖨 (to skip Print dialog box)	Click File, click Print (for Print dialog box)	[Ctrl]+[P] (for Print dialog box)

quiz

A. Identify Key Features

Name the items indicated by callouts in Figure 2-26.

Figure 2-26 Manipulating data in a worksheet

1. _____

2. _____

3. _____

4. _____

5. _____

6. _____

7. _____

8. _____

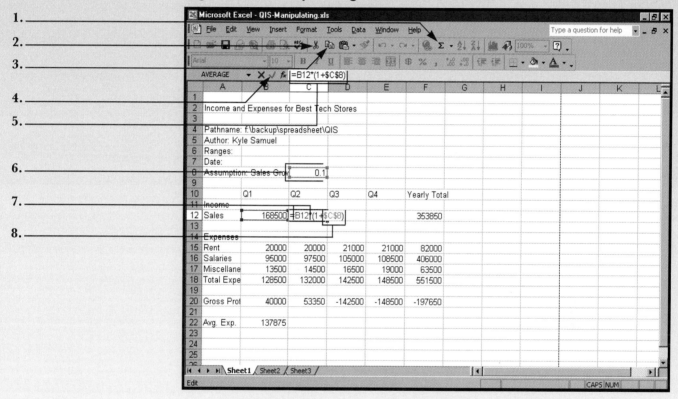

B. Select the Best Answer

9. Small square in the lower-right corner of an active cell

10. Temporary storage space for cut or copied information

11. Type this symbol to represent multiplication in a calculation

12. Allows you to see a worksheet as it will appear on a sheet of paper

13. Enables you to switch page orientation or adjust margins

14. Offers AVERAGE as one of its choices

15. Aligned to the right by default in Excel

16. Type this symbol to indicate absolute cell references

a. Values

b. Asterisk

c. Office Clipboard

d. Fill handle

e. Dollar sign

f. Insert Function dialog box

g. Print Preview mode

h. Page Setup dialog box

quiz (continued)

C. Complete the Statement

17. When you use the fill handle, cells to be filled are marked by a:

a. Gray border

b. Check mark

c. Plus sign

d. ScreenTip

18. Typing an apostrophe before a number instructs Excel to recognize it as a:

a. Formula

b. Function

c. Label

d. Value

19. None of the following actions will erase the Clipboard except:

a. Pasting an item

b. Cutting a new item

c. Copying a new item

d. Turning off the computer

20. By default, Excel considers formula cell references to be:

a. Absolute

b. AutoSums

c. Relative

d. Redundant

21. Changing conditions in one area of a worksheet to see how they affect calculations in another area is called:

a. Absolute analysis

b. Assumption analysis

c. What's-What Analysis

d. What-If Analysis

22. To copy cell contents to a new location, drag and drop the cell pointer while pressing:

a. [Ctrl]

b. [Enter]

c. [Shift]

d. [Tab]

23. An animated border indicates that the cell contents:

a. Are the result of a function or formula

b. Have been permanently deleted

c. Have been sent to the Office Clipboard

d. Have been pasted

24. Information enclosed in parentheses in a formula is called the:

a. Argument

b. Cell reference

c. Definition

d. Quantifier

25. Which of the following **could be** a correct order of operations in a formula?

a. Negation, Comparison, Multiplication, Addition

b. Negation, Percentage, Exponentiation, Multiplication

c. Comparison, Exponentiation, Addition, Multiplication

d. Addition, Subtraction, Multiplication, Division

26. The Print Preview toolbar has all of the following **except**:

a. A Zoom button

b. A Print button

c. A Setup button

d. A Page Orientation button

interactivity

Build Your Skills

1. Open a worksheet, cut and paste cell labels, and enter cell values:

   a. Open exskills2.xls and save it as ClassSked.xls.

   b. Cut and paste cells B2:B7 into cells A2:A7. Then cut and paste cells C3:C4 into cells B3:B4.

   c. Delete the contents of cell A7.

   d. Enter a number of hours, to the nearest half hour, for each activity in the cells matching the weekdays on which you do them. Do not fill in the totals.

   e. Resave the worksheet with the changes you have made.

2. Use AutoSum, the Insert Function, and the Fill Handle:

   a. Using AutoSum, calculate the total number of hours for Monday that you engage in all activities. Be sure you have accounted for all your time on Monday, so the total adds up to 24 hours.

   b. Using the fill handle, copy the AutoSum function for Monday into cells C17:F17.

   c. In cell G8, type the word Average. In cell G9 use the Insert Function command to calculate average hours spent per day on classes.

   d. Using the fill handle, copy the AVERAGE formula into cells G10:G16.

   e. Enter your name in cell A19, and enter the assignment date of this Skill in A20.

   f. Resave the worksheet with the changes you have made.

3. Preview and print the worksheet:

   a. Switch to Print Preview mode.

   b. Click the magnifying glass icon in the middle of the worksheet to enlarge the text size for easier viewing.

   c. Click the magnifying glass icon again to zoom back to the original view.

   d. Using the Print button on the Print Preview toolbar, print the worksheet.

   e. Click the Close button on the Print Preview toolbar to return to Normal view.

   f. Resave the worksheet with the changes you have made and close the file.

interactivity (continued)

Problem Solving Exercises

1. Open the file exproblem2-1.xls and save it as Revised HR Funds.xls. This worksheet will help you track a $16,000 annual human resources expense account to improve hiring rates. Cut and paste the documentation area into column A. Enter dollar amounts into the existing worksheet, staying under $4,000 per quarter. Add a Totals label at the bottom of the existing labels in column A. Use the new label to demonstrate that your monetary allotments do not exceed $4,000 per quarter. Use a formula to calculate the Quarter 1 Total. Use AutoFill to copy the formula into the remaining quarters. Use a function to calculate the Annual Total for Advertising. Use AutoFill to copy the formula into the remaining categories and the new Totals row. Enter your name and a due date in the proper documentation cells, resave, preview, and print the worksheet. Close the file.

2. Open the file exproblem2-2.xls, which is a blank schedule for keeping track of employee work hours. Save the file as Employee Schedule.xls. Using fictional names and hours for five to ten employees, complete the weekly employee schedule. Add a label to record the Total Weekly Hours for each employee. Add a label to record the Daily Totals for each employee and for all employees combined. Using the formula and function commands explained in this lesson, calculate the totals for the weekly hours and the daily hours. In the documentation area add your name and a due date to the appropriate cells. Resave, preview, print, and close the file.

3. Using the skills you have learned so far, create a new worksheet that will allow you to track your individual monthly expenses for the months of September through May. Save the file as Monthly Expenses.xls. In the top area of the worksheet, create a documentation area like the ones you have seen in the Lessons and end-of-chapter activities. In the bottom area of the worksheet, enter category labels such as Rent, Phone, Books/Supplies, Food, Recreation, and so on. Calculate your total expenses for each month, as well as your average monthly expenses over the nine months. Also include an assumption value of 5 percent to account for going over your allotted budget. Then conduct a What-If Analysis to recalculate your total and average expenses based on a 5 percent increase in one or two categories. Enter your name and an assignment due date in the proper cells of the documentation area. Resave, preview, print, and close the file.

4. Create the worksheet below; save it as Population.xls. Add a Totals row below the existing labels in column A. Use AutoSum to calculate the first decade of the Totals row, and use AutoFill to copy the formula to the appropriate cells. Insert a What-If percentage between 4% and 7% in cell B7, using it to recalculate each area's population growth for each decade, based on 1980 data. Add a name and due date in the proper cells. Resave, preview, print, and close the file.

Figure 2-27 Population.xls

	A	B	C	D	E	F	G
1							
2	Caribbean Population Trends						
3	Path name: f/backup/Stats/Population.xls						
4	Author: [Student Name]						
5	Ranges:						
6	Date: [Due Date]						
7	Population Growth:						
8							
9		1980	1990	2000	2010		
10	Antigua/Barbuda	60152	63555	66422			
11	The Bahamas	285012	290159	294982			
12	Barbados	264789	269874	274540			
13	Bermuda	60875	61200	62997			
14	Grenada	80569	82654	89018			
15	Jamaica	2158960	2254566	2652689			
16	Trinidad & Tobago	1053698	1105887	1175523			
17							

Formatting Worksheet Elements

Excel 2002 allows you to format the cells of your worksheets individually, format them as parts of rows and columns, format them automatically using the AutoFormat feature, and format them in ranges, or groups, of cells. Formatting refers to changing the appearance of information in a worksheet without changing the actual content of that information. You can use Excel's many formatting tools to improve the appearance and the readability of your worksheet. Text formatting includes font, font size, style, color, and alignment. You can format labels in a variety of styles, some of which help to express the kind of data that they represent. You also can format individual cells or ranges of cells. The AutoFormat command enables you to apply a set of predesigned formats to an entire range of cells at once.

Although the structure of an Excel worksheet is highly organized, it also is very flexible. You can restructure cells by merging them, or splitting previously merged cells. You can change the larger structure by increasing or decreasing column widths and row heights, or by adding or deleting rows and columns as needed. You even can maintain the overall structure of a worksheet, but hide (and then unhide) rows or columns when confidentiality or display needs dictate. When making changes to the structure of a worksheet, you first should decide what data needs to appear in the final worksheet and what formatting changes will enhance rather than muddle the worksheet's appearance.

You often will find that you are using a row or column of cells, or even a larger grouping of cells, that contains closely related data. Excel allows you to define these groups of related cells as ranges and then name them as you see fit. After naming the cell grouping, you then can locate that grouping immediately in the future and manage it or manipulate it as your needs and desires dictate.

Lesson Goal:

Format cells, cell values, and rows and columns. Manipulate rows and columns, and define and format cell ranges. Learn the advantages of AutoFormat.

skills

- Merging and Splitting Cells
- Formatting Cell Labels
- Formatting Cell Values
- Formatting Rows and Columns
- Inserting and Deleting Rows and Columns
- Hiding, Unhiding, and Protecting Cells
- Defining and Naming Cell Ranges
- Filling a Cell Range with Labels
- Applying Shading, Patterns, and Borders to Cells & Ranges
- Applying AutoFormat to a Worksheet

skill

Merging and Splitting Cells

concept

Excel 2002 allows you to format your cells by merging two or more cells into one cell or by splitting a merged cell back into the component cells of the worksheet. You may want to merge cells to ensure that a large amount of text fits in only one cell, to call attention to a part of the worksheet, or to consolidate data. You may want to split cells back into their component parts if you remove a large amount of text, eliminate something on the worksheet that previously required emphasis, need more cells for additional data, and so on.

do it !

Merge cells in order to enter longer text, and then split the merged cells to separate text from data.

1. Open Student File exdoit3-1.xls and save it as best-1.xls.

2. Click in cell A21 and drag through cell B21. Click Format, click Cells to open the Format Cells dialog box, and click the Alignment tab if needed to bring it forward. In the Text control section, add a check mark to the Merge cells check box (see Figure 3-1). Click the OK button ⬚ OK ⬚ to activate the merge and to close the dialog box.

3. With cells A21 and B21 now merged into cell A21 and still selected, click the Format Painter button 🖌 on the Standard toolbar. Click in cell A22 and drag through cell B22. The two selected cells in row 22 merge to match the format of merged cell A21. Press [Enter]. ⬤ Format Painter is handy tool for copying the formatting of one cell or cell range to another cell or cell range. Clicking the Format Painter button once enables you to copy a format of set of formats once. Clicking the button twice enables you to copy the format or formats repeatedly until you click the button again to turn the feature off.

4. In cell A21 type Average Sales/Qrtr. In cell A22 type Average Expenses/Qrtr. ⬤ You now could calculate the Average Sales and the Average Expenses by hand and type them into the relevant merged cells after adding a colon and a space to the abbreviation Qrtr in each row. However, doing so would contradict and defeat the formatting and formula capabilities of the worksheet. Therefore, you will split the merged cells and enter formulas in the restored column B cells for each category.

5. Click cell A21. Click Format, click Cells to open the Format Cells dialog box, and click the Alignment tab if needed to bring it forward. Click the Merge cells check box to remove the check mark that you placed there earlier, and click ⬚ OK ⬚. Repeat the same process in cell A22 by using either the Alignment tab or the Format Painter button. Rows 21 and 22 now have separate cells in columns A and B.

6. In cell B21 type the formula =average(B12:E12), then press [Enter]. In cell B22, use the AVERAGE function to calculate the average of cells B18:E18, then press [Enter]. Cells B21 and B22 now contain averages for, respectively, the quarterly sales and quarterly expenses that appear in the current worksheet (see Figure 3-2). ⬤ Instead of typing B12:E12 in the first formula, you could click in cell B12 and drag across into cell E12. This action identifies the selected cells as the desired range between the opening and closing parentheses of the formula.

7. Resave the worksheet with the changes you have made and close the file.

more

When you merge two or more cells, the cell reference for the merged area is the column letter and row number of the upper-left cell that was merged. Excel puts only the text and/or data from the upper-left cell into the merged area. If you had text and/or data in the other cells, Excel deletes that data from the merged cell. To change horizontal text alignment in the merged cell, click the Align Left 📄, Center 📄, or Align Right 📄 button on the Formatting toolbar. These buttons allow you to change the default alignment of labels and values. To change other features of text alignment (including vertical alignment) click Format, click Cells to open the Format Cells dialog box, click the Alignment tab to bring it forward, and use the options you need from the four sections of the tab. When you split a merged cell into its components, the Name box will display the cell reference of the upper-left cell from the latest merge, but the cell pointer border will surround all previously merged cells. To select a cell to type in, either click in the desired cell or press [Enter] until you see the desired cell reference in the Name box.

Figure 3-1 Alignment tab of Format Cells dialog box

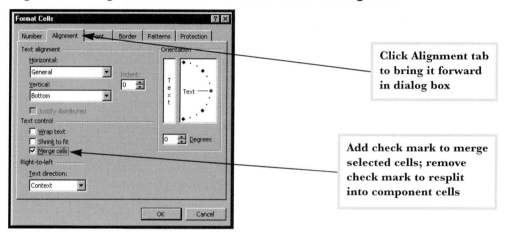

Click Alignment tab to bring it forward in dialog box

Add check mark to merge selected cells; remove check mark to resplit into component cells

Figure 3-2 Worksheet's appearance after merges, splits, and edits

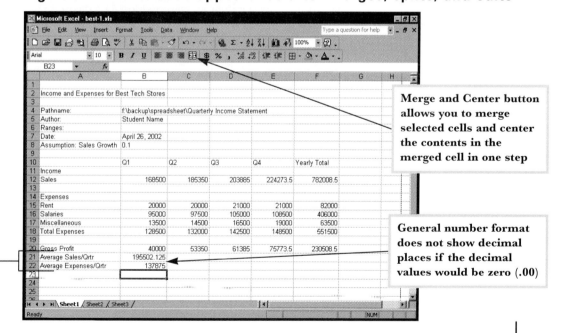

Merge and Center button allows you to merge selected cells and center the contents in the merged cell in one step

Merged and resplit cells

General number format does not show decimal places if the decimal values would be zero (.00)

Practice

To practice merging and splitting cells, follow the instructions on the Practice3-1 Sheet tab of the practice file exprac3.xls. Save changes as myexprac3-1.xls, and close the file.

skill Formatting Cell Labels

concept

Formatting cells enhances the appearance of your worksheet and makes the formatted cells stand out from the worksheet's default font so the formatted cells will be easier to read. Formatting options include changing the font style, font size, font color, text alignment, and similar cell characteristics. Before you can change the formatting of a cell or a group of cells (also called a range), you must select those cells.

do it !

Add formatting to cells to emphasize their importance to the worksheet.

1. Open Student File exdoit3-2.xls and save it as best-2.xls.

2. Click in cell A2 and drag into cell F2 to select cell range A2:F2. Click the Merge and Center button ⊞ on the Formatting toolbar. The six selected cells in row 2 merge into one cell. The worksheet title centers itself across all six columns, not just cell A2.

3. With cell A2 still highlighted, click Format, click Cells to open the Format Cells dialog box, and click the Font tab to bring it forward. In the scrollable box in the Font section, click Arial Black. In the scrollable box in the Size section, click 14 (see Figure 3-3). Click [OK] to apply the Font formats and to close the dialog box.

4. Click in cell A4 and drag into cell A8 to select the cell range A4:A8. With the cells selected, click the Bold button **B**. Position the mouse pointer over the right edge of the gray heading for column A so the pointer changes to ↔. Double-click to autofit the column to the width of the text in cell A8, which is slightly greater now that you have bolded it.

5. Click in cell B10 and drag into cell F10, then click the Center button ≡. With cells B10:F10 still highlighted, hold down [Ctrl] and click cells A11, A14, A18, and A20:A22. Release the [Ctrl] key without deselecting the nonadjacent cells. Click the Bold button **B**.

6. Click cell A11, hold down [Ctrl], and click cells A14, A18, and the cell range A20:A22. Click the Italic button *I*.

7. Click cell A2, hold down [Ctrl], select the cell range B10:F10 and the cell range A11:A22. Release [Ctrl] without deselecting the cells. Click the Font Color list button **A**▾ to display the 40 colored squares of the color palette below the button. Click the Dark Blue square in the first row, sixth column (see Figure 3-4). Click outside the selected cells to see that the font color has changed for the text of the worksheet title, the column headings for the four quarters and the Yearly Total, and the row headings in column A.

8. Click cell A12, hold down [Ctrl], and select the cell range A15:A17. Release [Ctrl] without deselecting the cells. Click the Increase Indent button ≣ to indent the text in the four selected cells slightly to the right (see Figure 3-5).

9. Resave the worksheet with the changes you have made and close the file.

more

The Font tab in the Format Cells dialog box allows you to change most text attributes. The options Font, Font style, and Size each have two boxes attached to them. The lower box is a list box that indexes available fonts, font styles, and font sizes, respectively. The upper box is a text box wherein you can enter any of these choices without having to scroll through a list in a lower box. However, the point size of your font selection is not limited to only those numbers listed, and can range anywhere between 1 and 409. The Underline option contains a drop-down list with five styles of underlines that you can use. The Color option contains a drop-down palette with 56 color choices. Clicking one of these boxes will change your text to that color. Checking the Normal font box reverts any changed font formats to the default settings. You also can select the following effects: Strikethrough draws a line through text, making it appear as crossed out; Superscript shrinks the text and raises it above the baseline; Subscript shrinks and drops the text below the baseline. Any time that you alter the format of a font using the dialog box, its altered look appears in the Preview window on the Font tab, and none of the alterations take effect on the worksheet until you close the dialog box.

Figure 3-3 Font tab of Format Cells dialog box

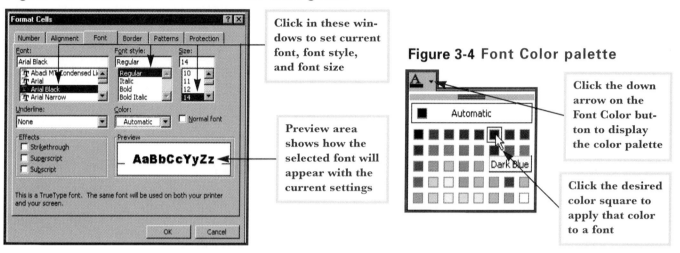

Figure 3-4 Font Color palette

Click in these windows to set current font, font style, and font size

Preview area shows how the selected font will appear with the current settings

Click the down arrow on the Font Color button to display the color palette

Click the desired color square to apply that color to a font

Figure 3-5 Worksheet's appearance after cell formats

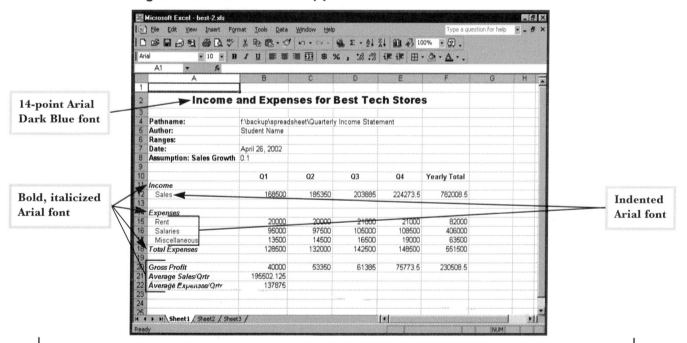

14-point Arial Dark Blue font

Bold, italicized Arial font

Indented Arial font

Practice

To practice formatting cell contents, follow the instructions on the Practice3-2 Sheet tab of the practice file exprac3.xls. Save changes as myexprac3-2.xls, and close the file.

skill

Formatting Cell Values

concept

Labels can help identify what kind of data a number represents. However, you still may want to format cell values themselves so that readers more readily understand what those values represent. Common formats include Currency, Percentage, Fraction, and Comma, all of which you can apply using toolbar buttons. Choose formats according to how you are using the values and how you wish them to look. You can apply cell or range formatting before or after you enter data, but you can choose formats more easily and intelligently if the values to which you apply those formats already appear in the worksheet.

do it !

Format all values with commas for easier reading, format the first and last lines of dollar amounts in Currency style, format the assumption in Percentage style, and remove the decimal places in selected cells.

1. Open Student File exdoit3-3.xls and save it as best-3.xls. Review the Formatting toolbar in Figure 3-6.

2. Select the cell range B12:F22. Click the Comma Style button ⟦,⟧. All of the cells contained within the selected range will be formatted in the Comma Style, which includes two decimal places.

3. Select the cell range B12:F12. While holding down [Ctrl], also select the cell range B20:F20. Release [Ctrl] without deselecting the cells. Click the Currency Style button ⟦$⟧. The values in the selected cells will appear with dollar signs at the left margin of the cells and two decimal places now will represent cents.

4. Select cell B8, which contains the value 0.1. Click the Percent Style button ⟦%⟧. The value will now appear as 10%. The result of the formula whose argument references this cell will remain the same.

5. Select the cell range B21:B22. Click the Currency Style button ⟦$⟧ , then click Decrease Decimal button ⟦.00→.0⟧ twice. The two decimal places in the selected cells will disappear (see Figure 3-7).

6. Resave the worksheet with the changes you have made and close the file.

more

When you applied the Currency, Comma, and Percentage styles to the worksheet, you used the default style for each of these buttons. However, you can apply many more styles for 12 different categories of values by using the Numbers tab of the Format Cells dialog box. To access this tab, click Format, click Cells to open the dialog box, and click the Number tab if needed to bring it forward. In the Category section on the left side of the tab, click the name of the value that you need to format—for example, Currency, Date, Time, Fraction, and so on. After choosing a Category, click in the Type section on the right side of the dialog box for a specific style. Some values have just one box in the type section for formatting options. Other values, like Currency, allow you to choose how many decimals to display, to display a symbol such as a dollar sign, and to select a format for negative numbers.

When choosing a Category, be sure it relates to the type of data you are formatting. Don't select just the Number category, for example, to format Date or Time. When choosing a format in the Type section, be sure it is specific enough to represent the selected values adequately. For example, a worksheet for calculating weekly personal expenses probably should include two decimals to display cents. However, a worksheet for displaying annual corporate earnings can be rounded off to whole dollars.

Figure 3-6 Formatting toolbar

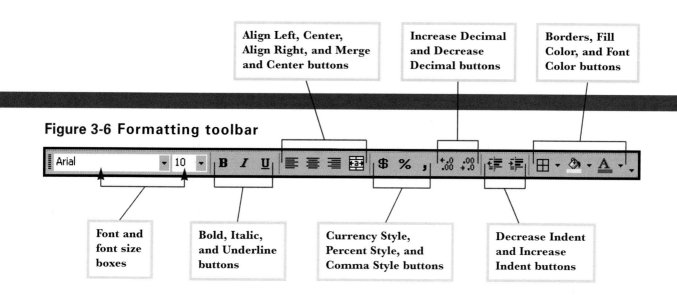

Align Left, Center, Align Right, and Merge and Center buttons

Increase Decimal and Decrease Decimal buttons

Borders, Fill Color, and Font Color buttons

Font and font size boxes

Bold, Italic, and Underline buttons

Currency Style, Percent Style, and Comma Style buttons

Decrease Indent and Increase Indent buttons

Figure 3-7 Worksheet's appearance after formatting cell values

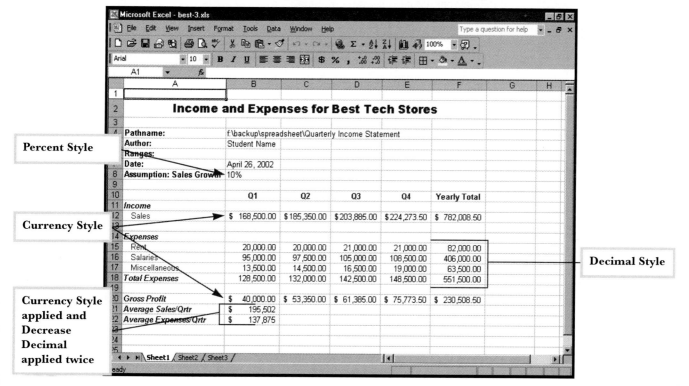

Percent Style

Currency Style

Decimal Style

Currency Style applied and Decrease Decimal applied twice

Practice

To practice formatting cell values, follow the instructions on the Practice3-3 Sheet tab of the practice file exprac3.xls. Save changes as myexprac3-3.xls, and close the file.

skill Formatting Rows and Columns

concept

Sometimes the information you enter in a worksheet will not fit neatly into a cell that is set with the default height and width. Other times, you may encounter a worksheet prepared by someone else who did not format it very well, and you may have to reformat it somewhat before working with it further. In these cases, you may need to adjust the height of a row or, more commonly, the width of a column. Standard column width is 8.43 characters, but can be set anywhere between 0 and 255.

do it !

Widen some columns to accommodate long labels and values and restore default row heights.

1. Open Student File exdoit3-4.xls and save it as best-4.xls. Notice that column A is too narrow to display all the text in cells A8, A21, and A22, and that the text in cell F10 is cut off at the beginning and runs into column G. Notice that rows 11, 14, 18, and 20 are twice the height of the other rows in the worksheet, forcing part of the worksheet below the bottom of the worksheet window (depending on your screen resolution settings).

2. Click the gray heading for column A to select the entire column. A down-pointing black arrow [↓] will appear when the mouse pointer is over the column heading. Click Format, click Column, and click Width to display the Column Width dialog box with the Column width text box already highlighted. Type 25 (see Figure 3-8). Click [OK] to change the width of column A and to close the dialog box. To display the Column Width dialog box, you also could right-click the heading of row A to display a shortcut menu, and then click the Column Width command.

3. Position the mouse pointer on the right edge of the gray heading for column F so that the pointer changes to ↔. Double-click to autofit column F, expanding the column to a width that will accommodate the contents of cell F10.

4. Click the heading for row 11, hold down [Ctrl], and click the headings for rows 14, 18, and 20. All four row headings and all the cells in the rows will highlight, just as they did when you selected column headings. Without deselecting the four rows, click the bottom edge of the heading for row 20 and hold down the mouse button to display a ScreenTip showing the current row height. While holding down the mouse button, carefully drag the bottom edge of row 20 upward until the ScreenTip reads Height: 12.75 (17 pixels), as shown in Figure 3-9, then release the mouse button. All four selected rows return to their default height.

5. Click the heading of row 12, hold down [Ctrl], and click the headings for rows 15 through 17. Click the Italic button [*I*]. All labels and data in the four rows will appear italicized (see Figure 3-10). Because you highlighted the row headings, not just some row cells, anything typed in any column of the four selected rows would appear italicized.

6. Resave the worksheet with the changes you have made and close the file.

more

The Steps above demonstrate that you have three ways to adjust row height or column width: (1) click and drag the right edge of the column heading or bottom edge of the row heading until you see in the ScreenTip the desired size of the row or column, (2) click the row or column heading, click Format, and click Row or Column to display the dialog box in which to enter a number, or (3) right-click on the row or column heading, click Row Height or Column Width to display the dialog box in which to enter a number. To widen several rows or columns at once, select the rows or columns to be changed, then drag any selected row or column edge as desired. To widen all rows or columns at once, click the Select All button ☐ (to the left of the column A header, click Format, click Row or Column, and then click Height or Width to open the dialog box in which to enter a number. Remember, however, that you usually do not need to change row height manually, as Excel adjusts row height to fit the largest point size of a cell's label or data.

ScreenTips that display when you drag a column indicate the number of characters that will fit in the column, with the size of a character being equal to the average size of the digits 0-9. On a standard worksheet the default column width is 8.43 digits (64 pixels). Row height is measured in points. For a standard worksheet, which uses 10-point Arial font, the default row height is 12.75 points (17 pixels). Since there are 72 points in an inch, the font is slightly smaller than 1/7 of an inch and the row height is slightly larger, providing some white space above and below the text.

Figure 3-8 Column Width dialog box

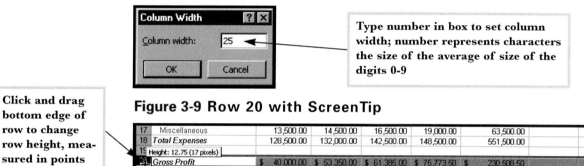

Type number in box to set column width; number represents characters the size of the average of size of the digits 0-9

Click and drag bottom edge of row to change row height, measured in points

Figure 3-9 Row 20 with ScreenTip

17	Miscellaneous	13,500.00	14,500.00	16,500.00	19,000.00	63,500.00
18	Total Expenses	128,500.00	132,000.00	142,500.00	148,500.00	551,500.00
19	Height: 12.75 (17 pixels)					
20	Gross Profit	$ 40,000.00	$ 53,350.00	$ 61,385.00	$ 75,773.50	$ 230,508.50
21	Average Sales/Qrtr	$ 195,502				
22	Average Expenses/Qrtr	$ 137,875				
23						

Figure 3-10 Worksheet's appearance after row and column formatting

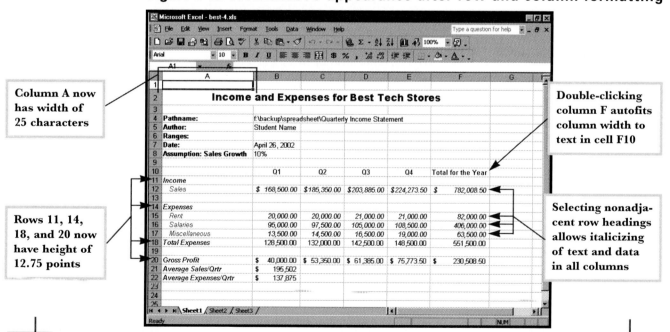

Column A now has width of 25 characters

Rows 11, 14, 18, and 20 now have height of 12.75 points

Double-clicking column F autofits column width to text in cell F10

Selecting nonadjacent row headings allows italicizing of text and data in all columns

Practice

To practice formatting rows and columns, follow the instructions on the Practice3-4 Sheet tab of the practice file exprac3.xls. Save changes as myexprac3-4.xls, and close the file.

skill

Inserting and Deleting Rows and Columns

MOUS Skill

concept

In Excel you can add and delete rows and columns to customize worksheets to meet specific needs. In a personal expenses worksheet, you might add a row to display expenses for a newly acquired car. In a business worksheet you might add more rows when you hire additional employees. You might add six monthly columns to convert from a half-year to full-year worksheet, or delete unneeded columns just to create a more tightly formatted worksheet.

do it !

Insert one row between the documentation section and the main body of the worksheet, insert rows near the bottom, and delete a blank column near the right side of the worksheet,

1. Open Student File exdoit3-5.xls and save it as best-5.xls. Notice the blank column F near the right side of the worksheet.

2. Click on cell A9. Click Insert, then click the Cells command. The Insert dialog box will open with the Shift cells down option button selected.

3. Click the Entire row option button. This button tells Excel to add a row and shift down all of the rows from row 9 and below (see Figure 3-11). Click [OK]. A new row will be inserted, the main body of the worksheet will shift down by one row, and your formulas will update to reflect the row shift. Ignore the Insert Options Smart Tag, if it appears.

4. Select the gray headings of rows 22 through 24. Click Insert, then click Rows (see Figure 3-12). Excel inserts three blank rows immediately above the three rows with text and data that you selected and renumbers the rows that moved down.

5. In cell A23 type Gross Profit Margin. In cell B23, type the formula =B21/B13 and press [Enter]. Position the mouse pointer over the fill handle in the lower-right corner of cell B23. When the mouse pointer converts to a black cross ✚, drag into cell G23 to copy the formula into the cells you selected. With cell range B23:G23 still selected, click the Percent Style button %. Ignore the formula error in cell F23, since you will delete column F shortly. ◗ Since there was no data in cell F23, Excel automatically displayed the #DIV/0! error, which appears when a cell tries to divide any number by zero.

6. Right-click on the gray heading of column F to display a shortcut menu. Click the Delete command (see Figure 3-13), removing column F and moving the text and data of column G into column F (see Figure 3-14).

7. Resave the worksheet with the changes you have made and close the file.

more

Step 4 shows you how to insert several adjacent rows at once into a worksheet. To insert several adjacent columns at once, you must select the same number of columns immediately to the right of where you want to insert the columns. After selecting the rows or columns, click Insert, then click Rows or Columns accordingly as needed. When you insert or delete rows, Excel updates formulas by adjusting references to shifted cells to account for their new location. However, new rows or columns sometimes can create problems for formulas that reference data that is adjacent to those new areas. Suppose you add a row or column at the end of a cell range—a group of related cells—that appears in a formula. In that case, you must change the formula to account for the new row or column. To avoid having to edit such a formula, include a dummy row or column at the end of, but still inside, the range that is referenced by the formula. If you then insert another row or column of data into the range, the formula automatically will change to include the new data.

Deleting a row or column can create problems for formulas that used to reference data in the deleted row or column. Suppose that you delete a row or column and then a formula in the worksheet displays the #REF error value. In this case, you have deleted one or more cells that contained data referenced by the formula. When inserting or deleting rows or columns, therefore, review the location and contents of formulas before and after a change to see if the formulas calculate data correctly.

Figure 3-11 Insert dialog box   Figure 3-12 Inserting rows   Figure 3-13 Deleting a column

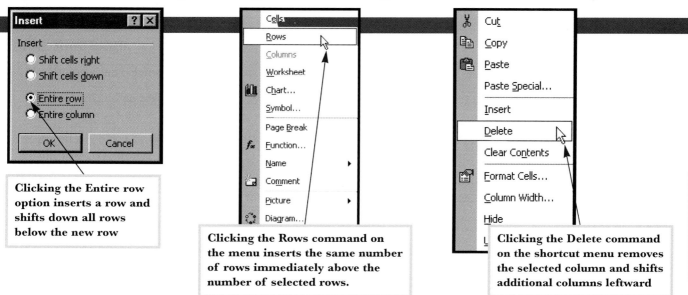

Clicking the Entire row option inserts a row and shifts down all rows below the new row

Clicking the Rows command on the menu inserts the same number of rows immediately above the number of selected rows.

Clicking the Delete command on the shortcut menu removes the selected column and shifts additional columns leftward

Figure 3-14 Worksheet's appearance after insertions and deletions

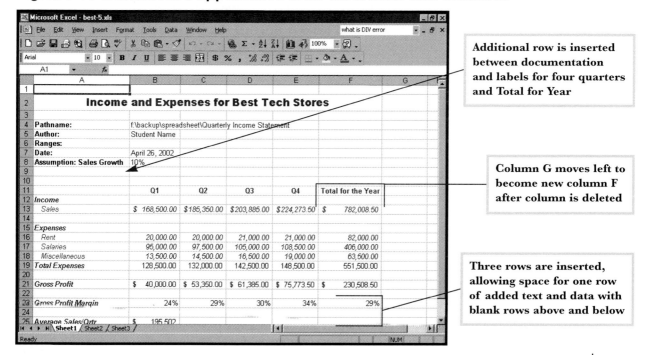

Additional row is inserted between documentation and labels for four quarters and Total for Year

Column G moves left to become new column F after column is deleted

Three rows are inserted, allowing space for one row of added text and data with blank rows above and below

Practice

To practice inserting and deleting rows and columns, follow the instructions on the Practice3-5 Sheet tab of the practice file exprac3.xls. Save changes as myexprac3-5.xls, and close the file.

skill Hiding, Unhiding, and Protecting Cells

concept

Excel allows you to hide and unhide rows and columns and to protect many elements of a worksheet or workbook. You may want to hide worksheet elements that include confidential data or hide them simply to create a smaller worksheet, perhaps, for printing purposes. You can unhide those elements later for everyone or for just those with access rights to the data. For similar security reasons you protect worksheets and lock sensitive cells and then unprotect them and unlock them later as needed.

do it !

Hide two rows and one column and print the worksheet, then unhide the rows and column. Protect the worksheet so it cannot be changed, and then unprotect it to regain editing access.

1. Open Student File exdoit3-6.xls and save it as best-6.xls.

2. In order to create a smaller worksheet for printing purposes, you decide to hide two rows and one column of the worksheet. If necessary, scroll down slightly to display rows 25 and 26 of the worksheet. Click the gray heading for row 25 to select the entire row and drag into row 26 to select it too. Click Format, click Row, and click Hide (see Figure 3-15). The two selected rows now are hidden. Notice that the heading numbers for rows 25 and 26 are missing in the sequence of row numbers at the left edge of the worksheet window.

3. Right-click the gray heading for column F. On the shortcut menu that appears, click Hide (see Figure 3-16). Column F now is hidden. Notice that the heading letter for column F is missing in the sequence of column letters at the top edge of the worksheet window.

4. Verify that your worksheet resembles Figure 3-17. Resave the worksheet, and click the Print button 🖨. All of the unhidden rows and columns should display on a print-out whether you print in Portrait or Landscape orientation. If you need help printing the worksheet, consult the Skill "Previewing and Printing a Worksheet" in Lesson 2 or "Using Advanced Printing Features" in Lesson 4.

5. Click in the heading of row 24 and drag into the heading of row 27 to select the rows immediately above and below the rows that you hid in Step 2. Click Format, click Row, and click Unhide on the submenu to unhide rows 25 and 26.

6. Click the heading of column E and drag into the heading of column G to select the columns immediately to the left and right of the column that you hid in Step 3. Right-click to display a shortcut menu and click Unhide to unhide column F.

(continued on EX 3.14)

Figure 3-15 Hide Row command

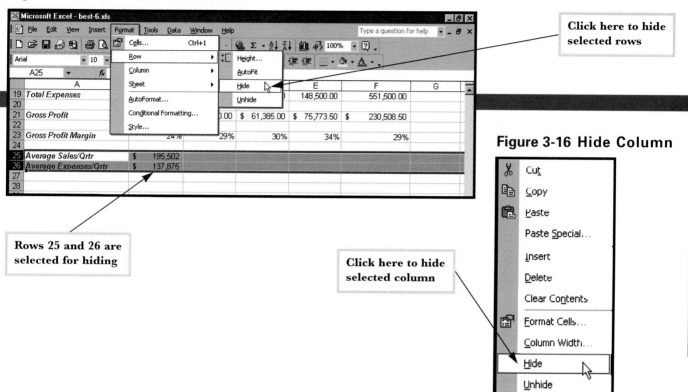

Click here to hide selected rows

Rows 25 and 26 are selected for hiding

Figure 3-16 Hide Column

Click here to hide selected column

Figure 3-17 Worksheet with hidden rows and column

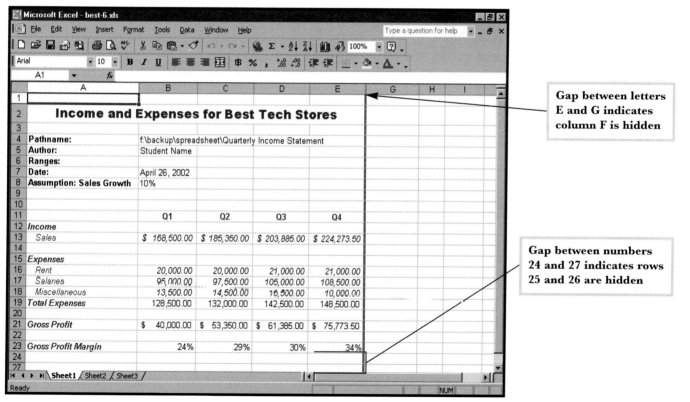

Gap between letters E and G indicates column F is hidden

Gap between numbers 24 and 27 indicates rows 25 and 26 are hidden

skill   Hiding, Unhiding, and Protecting Cells (continued)

do it !

7. Click in cell A1 or press [Ctrl]+[Home] to place the cell pointer in the upper left cell of the worksheet. Click Tools, click Protection, and click Protect Sheet on the submenu to display the Protect Sheet dialog box (see Figure 3-18). Be sure a check mark appears in the Protect worksheet and contents of locked cells check box. Do **not** type a password in the Password to unprotect sheet text box. Click [OK] to protect the worksheet and to close the dialog box.

8. Click in any cell that contains text or a value on the worksheet. Try to type anything into the selected cell. A Microsoft Excel warning box will appear to advise you that your worksheet is protected and to explain how to unprotect it. When you have finished reading the box, click [OK]. Then, click Tools, click Protection, and click Unprotect Sheet on the submenu to regain editing access to the worksheet (see Figure 3-19).

9. Resave the worksheet and close the file.

more

In this Skill you hid and unhid rows that had an accessible row above them, and you hid and unhid columns that had an accessible column to their left. But what do you do when you need to unhide row 1 or Column A? To unhide these areas, click Edit, click Go To to display the Go To dialog box, type A1 in the Reference text box, and click [OK]. Then click Format, click Row or Column, and then click Unhide. Alternately, you can unhide row 1 just by clicking and dragging down the top edge of row 2, and you can unhide column A by clicking and dragging the left edge of column B to the right. When unhiding these areas in these simpler ways, be sure that you know what height or width the row or column should be restored to.

The purposes of this Skill do not require you to create a password in the Protect Sheet dialog box. If using a password, however, make it hard for others to guess at, but easy for you to remember. For example, avoid passwords like Excel-123 in favor of ones like eXce123-, in which the second letter is the only capital, the number "1" replaces the letter "l" from the name of the program, and the hyphen has been moved to the unlikely end position. Passwords in this dialog box are case sensitive, requiring you to remember what combination of capital and lowercase letters you used when you most recently created them. Excel passwords can use any letters, numbers, and symbols and—although not usually needed—can run up to 255 characters. To password-protect all worksheets in a workbook, click File, click Save As, click Tools, click General Options to open the Save Options dialog box, enter your desired passwords, and click [OK]. Alternatively, click Tools, click Protection, click Protect Workbook to open the Protect Workbook dialog box, complete the desired options, and click [OK].

Besides protecting worksheets or whole workbooks to prohibit altering their text and data, you also can lock selected cells. When you do so, others can see your text or data but cannot change it. To lock or unlock cells, click Format, click Cells to open the Format Cells dialog box, click the Protection tab to bring it forward, and add or remove a check mark in the Locked check box. By default Excel locks the cells in a standard worksheet, but the locking mode does not work unless you also protect the worksheet, as the Skill above demonstrates. To lock parts of a worksheet (e.g., its formulas) while leaving other areas unlocked (e.g., data-entry cells), unlock only those cells to which others need access while leaving all other cells locked, then protect the sheet as described in the Skill above.

Figure 3-18 Protect Sheet dialog box

Turns protection of work-
sheet cells on and changes
to locked cells on or off

Entering a password prevents
unauthorized users from
unprotecting a worksheet

Select options you
want to activate for
all worksheet users

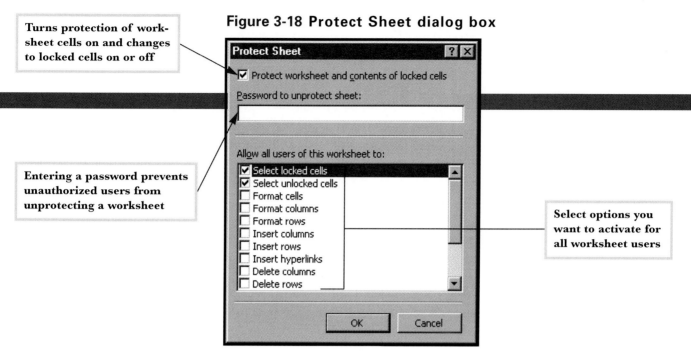

Figure 3-19 Unprotect Sheet command

Column F is unhidden
after Step 6

Click to regain editing
access to worksheet

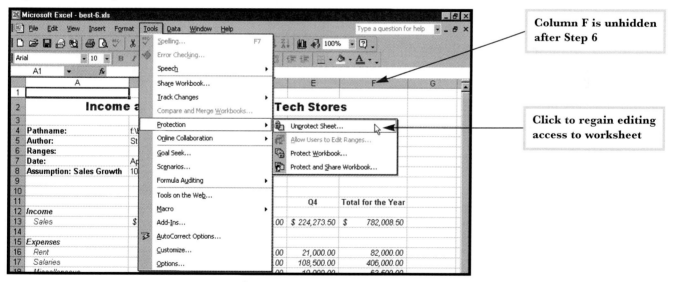

Practice

To practice hiding, unhiding, and protecting cells, follow the instructions on the Practice3-6 Sheet tab
of the practice file exprac3.xls. Save changes as myexprac3-6.xls, and close the file.

skill   Defining and Naming Cell Ranges

concept

Excel allows you to define and name a range of cells. A name is a string of characters, usually a word, representing a cell, a cell range, a formula, or a constant. A range is a group of cells, usually adjacent and usually referring to a related type of information or data such as book titles or employee names or inventory items. By naming a range, you can access that range just by clicking its name in the Name box and then format, edit, or otherwise modify or manipulate the range. You also can use range names in formulas instead of typing complicated cell references. Naming ranges, therefore, saves time and simplifies working with data.

do it !

Define and name cell ranges in a worksheet that contain data.

1. Open Student File exdoit3-7.xls and save it as best-7.xls.

2. Select cells B13 through E13 to define and highlight the range for Sales as B13:E13. Click inside the Name box [B13] to the left of the Formula bar. Type Sales, and press [Enter]. You now have named the range B13:E13 as Sales (see Figure 3-20). Whenever you click on the word Sales in the name box, cells B13:E13 will highlight on the worksheet. Whenever you select cells B13:E13 on the worksheet, the name Sales will appear in the Name box.

3. Repeat Step 2 to name the remaining cell ranges. Be sure to press [Enter] after you type in each name. Type Rent for the range B16:E16. Type Salaries for B17:E17. Type Miscellaneous for B18:E18. Type Total_Expenses for B19:E19. Type Gross_Profit for B21:E21. Type Gross_Profit_Margin for B23:E23. Range names cannot contain spaces, so be sure to use an underscore ([Shift]+[-]) between the words Total and Expenses, between Gross and Profit, and among the words Gross, Profit, and Margin.

4. Select cells B12 through B23 to define and highlight the range for Q1 (or Quarter 1) as B13:B23. Click Insert, click Name, and click Define, as shown in Figure 3-21, to open the Define Name dialog box. Replace Q1 with Quarter_1 (including the underscore), and press [Enter] to name the range and to close the dialog box. Excel automatically picks up a column or row label as the default range name if it adjoins or appears in the selected range, so Q1 appears by default in the Names in workbook text box. However, this combination also represents column Q, row 1, and cannot be accepted.

5. Repeat Step 4, using the Define Name dialog box, to name the cell ranges for the three remaining Quarters. For C12:C23, name the cell range as Quarter_2. For D12:D23, name the cell range as Quarter_3. For E12:E23, name the cell range as Quarter_4 (see Figure 3-22). After closing the dialog box, click outside of all of the Quarter columns to cancel the selection of the last range named in the Step above.

6. Resave the worksheet with the changes you have made and close the file.

more

Ranges do not have to be made up of cells that touch. They can contain nonadjacent blocks of cells, or many nonadjoining individual cells. To name a nonadjacent range, (1) select the first cell or group of cells you wish to include, (2) hold down [Ctrl] while selecting the second and any additional cells or cell clusters to include in the range, and (3) name the range in the Name box to the left of the Formula bar. You can select as many nonadjacent cells or ranges as needed. Clicking outside of the selected cells cancels the selection.

Figure 3-20 B13:E13 as cell range named Sales

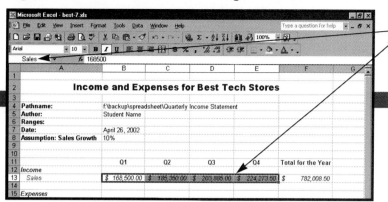

Selecting cell range name in Name box highlights related cell range; selecting cell range displays range name in Name box

Figure 3-21 Define command on submenu

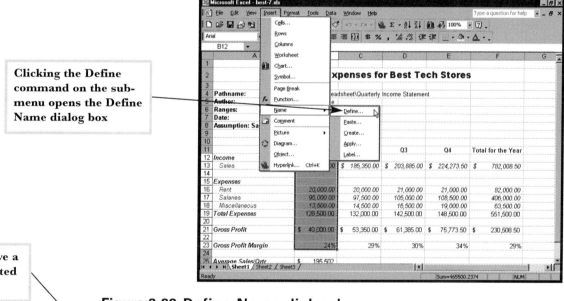

Clicking the Define command on the sub-menu opens the Define Name dialog box

Type here to give a name to a selected cell range

Click a name here to appear in Names in workbook text box

Displays worksheet number and cell range for the name appearing in Names in workbook text box

Figure 3-22 Define Name dialog box

Click to add a selected range name to the list of names defined for the workbook

Click to delete a selected range name

Practice

To practice defining and naming cell ranges, follow the instructions on the Practice3-7 Sheet tab of the practice file exprac3.xls. Save changes as myexprac3-7.xls, and close the file.

skill

Filling a Cell Range with Labels

concept

Excel can automatically fill a cell range with several types of series information. Series information includes numbers, text and numbers (e.g., Quarter 1), dates, and times. Excel can step, or increase, a series by a constant set value or multiply by a constant factor. For example, you can add all of the months of the year to a worksheet by typing only the word January and then extending the series. Before you fill a cell range, be sure you know what values should appear in that range and how large an increase should occur cell by cell.

do it !

Delete the Q1, Q2, Q3, Q4 series and use the AutoFill feature to insert a new series.

1. Open Student File exdoit3-8.xls and save it as best-8.xls.

2. Select cells B11:E11, and then press [Delete] to remove the text from all of the cells.

3. Click cell B11, and type Quarter 1.

4. Position the mouse pointer ⌖ over the fill handle (small black box) in the lower-right corner of cell B11 until the pointer changes to a small black cross ✚.

5. While holding down the mouse button, drag the fill handle to the right into cell E11. As you drag the fill handle, a border will appear, indicating the cells that you have selected. ScreenTips will appear to show what text will go in the cell where the fill handle currently resides (see Figure 3-23).

6. When you have finished filling cells B11:E11, release the mouse button. An AutoFill Options button also will appear at the right end of cell E11.The range that previously read Q1, Q2, Q3, Q4 now reads Quarter 1, Quarter 2, Quarter 3, and Quarter 4. If needed, click a blank cell and press [Delete] to close the AutoFill Options button.

7. Resave the worksheet with the changes you have made and close the file.

more

In Steps 4 and 5 above, you used AutoFill to enter a series of labels into a range of cells. Along with AutoFill, there are three other series fill types that you can use: Linear, Growth, and Date. These are advanced options and appear in the Series dialog box (see Figure 3-24). To access this dialog box, click Edit, click Fill, and click Series on the submenu. A Linear series fill, with the Trend box unchecked, adds the Step value to the value in the selected cell. With the Trend box checked, Excel disregards the Step value and calculates the trend based on the average of the difference between the values in the selected cells. Excel then uses this average to fill the range by increasing or decreasing the value by a constant amount. If necessary, the original selected cell information is replaced to fit the trend. A Growth series fill resembles a Linear series fill, except that Excel multiplies numbers to create a geometric growth trend instead of adding values. A Date series fill is based upon dates using the options in the Date unit list. You can extend selected dates by day, weekday, month, or year. You can set the Stop value to fix a value at which the series will end. If Excel fills a selected range before it reaches the Stop value, the values increase no further and do not try to reach the Stop value.

Right-clicking a selected cell displays the normal worksheet shortcut menu to cut, copy, paste, and otherwise manipulate cells. If you select a value, right-click the fill handle, drag it, and release it in a new cell, a shortcut menu appears that allows you to choose a series type to insert into the destination cells. These Excel features have been available for some time. However, as Step 6 indicates, the normal use of the fill handle now displays an AutoFill Options button, which is new to Excel in this version of the program. The AutoFill Options button enables you to copy cell values instead of autofilling the series, use the normal autofill, autofill with the formatting of the original cells, and autofill without that formatting.

Figure 3-23 Filling a cell range with labels

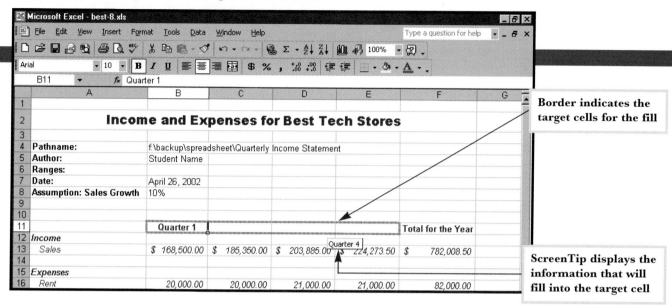

Border indicates the target cells for the fill

ScreenTip displays the information that will fill into the target cell

Click to select whether series fills across selected rows or down selected columns

Click the type of series that you want to fill

Figure 3-24 Series dialog box

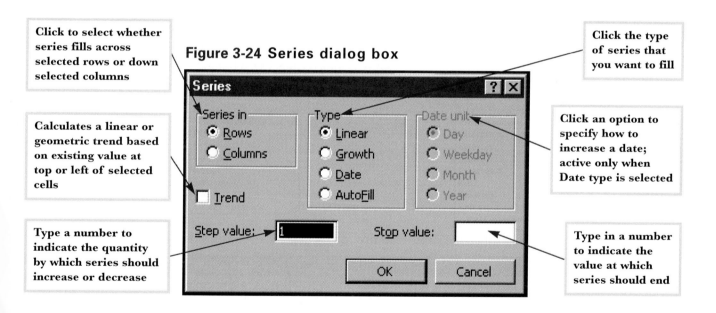

Calculates a linear or geometric trend based on existing value at top or left of selected cells

Click an option to specify how to increase a date; active only when Date type is selected

Type a number to indicate the quantity by which series should increase or decrease

Type in a number to indicate the value at which series should end

Practice

To practice filling a cell range with labels, follow the instructions on the Practice3-8 Sheet tab of the practice file exprac3.xls. Save changes as myexprac3-8.xls, and close the file.

skill
Applying Shading, Patterns, and Borders to Cells & Ranges

concept

As previous Skills have shown, you can format the look of and data in worksheet cells to make the worksheet more attractive and understandable. The AutoFormat command, which appears in the next Skill, enables you to apply a predefined set of formatting characteristics to a worksheet and then to modify that set slightly. Sometimes, however, you may want to have more precise control over the appearance of a cell or cell range. Excel therefore enables you to fill cells and ranges with colors and patterns and to outline them with special borders.

do it !

Add a color pattern and a border to the title and heading labels of a worksheet.

1. Open Student File exdoit3-9.xls and save it as best-9.xls.

2. Click cell A2 to select the merged and centered cell containing the worksheet's title. Hold down [Ctrl], select cells B11:F11 as well, and release [Ctrl]. Click the list arrow on the right edge of the Fill Color button ⬛▾ to display a color palette. Click the Light Green color square in the fifth row, fourth column of the palette. The palette will close and the selected cells will be filled with Light Green.

3. With the title cell and cells B11:F11 still selected, click Format, then click Cells to open the Format Cells dialog box. Click the Border tab to bring it to the front of the dialog box.

4. In the Line Style section, click the dashed line, which is the fourth line down in the second column. Click the Color selection arrow to display a color palette, and click the Dark Teal square from the first row, fifth column. In the Presets section click the Outline button (see Figure 3-25).

5. Click the Patterns tab to bring it forward. Notice that the Light Green color is selected in the color palette and appears in the Sample box because you already applied that color to the selected cell.

6. Click the Pattern selection arrow to display a color palette that includes patterns at the top. Click the Thin Diagonal Stripe pattern in the third row, fourth column. Click [OK] to apply the color and border (see Figure 3-26). View the formatted worksheet (see Figure 3-27). Click outside the selected cells to cancel the selection. ⬛ Although some people might have a slight difficulty viewing this pattern, the diagonal stripes look less intrusive when printed on paper. Make it a habit, therefore, to test print a page before submitting a final copy at school or work.

7. Resave the worksheet with the changes you have made and close the file.

more

The Font Color, Fill Color, and Borders buttons are all "loaded" with the most recent color or border type that you have applied, which is displayed as part of the button's icon. To apply the same color or border more than once, you do not need to click the button's arrow and open a palette. Simply click on the button itself and Excel will apply the most recent color or border that you chose. Also remember to use colors, patterns, and borders carefully. Some color shades may look light on a color screen but will print darkly on a black-and-white printer. The hue, or tint, of colors also may look different on paper than they did on the screen. Overusing colors or combining colors in a garish or cartoonish way will make your worksheets less attractive and harder to read. In these situations, therefore, aim for simplicity and consistency of appearance.

Figure 3-25 Border tab

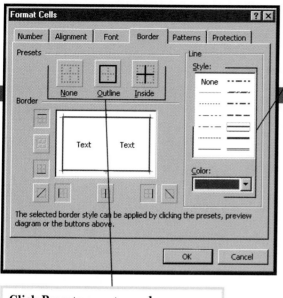

Click to select line weight and style, then click list arrow and select color for border to be applied

Click Presets area to apply or remove internal or external borders, or click options surrounding Preview area to choose individual borders

Figure 3-26 Patterns tab

Click in Color area to select background color, then in Pattern area for background pattern and pattern color

Sample area shows how selected cells will look with chosen color and/or pattern

Figure 3-27 Worksheet formatted with border, shading, and pattern

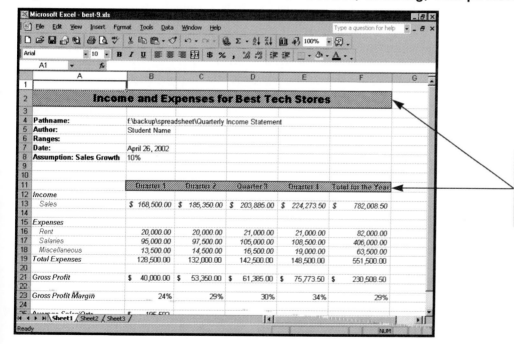

Light Green background, Dark Teal border, and Thin Diagonal Stripe pattern applied to selected cells

Practice

To practice applying shading, patterns, and borders, follow the instructions on the Practice3-9 Sheet tab of the practice file exprac3.xls. Save two files as directed in the Practice tab instructions, and close the files.

skill | Applying AutoFormat to a Worksheet

concept

Although Excel has many formatting options, sometimes you may want to format a worksheet all at once with Excel's AutoFormat command—a preset collection of format characteristics like font, font size, shadings, borders, and alignments that you can apply to a few cells or to an entire worksheet. When you choose an AutoFormat option, Excel identifies the worksheet's categories and data details and makes an assumption as to where to apply formats. Even after using AutoFormat, therefore, you may want to slightly adjust the formats that display.

do it !

Use the AutoFormat command to improve the appearance of a worksheet and to set the main body of data off from the documentation.

1. Open exdoit3-10.xls and save it as best-10.xls. The data previously in rows 25 and 26 is gone since such data, although informative, usually does not appear in income statements.

2. Click in cell A2 and drag into row 8. ⬡ Because cell A2 is merged all the way to column F, the dragging action selects all the way to that column in the lower rows as well. Since no text or data in the lower rows extends beyond column F, all of the information will be included in the selection.

3. Click Format, then click AutoFormat to open the AutoFormat dialog box. Click the Simple worksheet style in row 1, column 1 (see Figure 3-28). Click [OK] to apply the worksheet style and to close the dialog box. This worksheet style (1) changes the font of the title, (2) widens column B to hold all of the text in cell B4, (3) aligns the date and Sales Growth percent to the right in cells B7 and B8, respectively, and (4) adds three horizontal borders.

4. Select cells A11:F23. Click Format, click AutoFormat, and click the Simple worksheet style again. Click [OK] to apply the style and close the dialog box. This style (1) removes the italics from column A but bolds the text in cells A12, A13, A15, A19, A21, and A23, (2) narrows column B to match the width of the data in cell B13, which is the widest cell in the lower area of the whole worksheet, and (3) adds eleven horizontal borders. ⬡ The AutoFormat command offers some distinctive and colorful worksheet styles. However, as the previous Skill suggests, you generally should choose simpler styles, especially for work assignments or for situations in which you have only a black-and-white printer.

5. Notice that cell A8 is too narrow to display all of its text. Double-click the right edge of column A to autofit the column to the width of that cell. Also, the subcategory Sales under the category Income is bold while the three subcategories under the category Expenses are not. Click cell A13, and click the Bold button ⬚B to remove the bold style in that cell (see Figure 3-29).

6. Resave the worksheet with the changes you have made and close the file.

more

As Steps 2 and 4 indicate, you must select a range of cells before you can specify and apply an AutoFormat in the AutoFormat dialog box. The dialog box offers 16 AutoFormat options and a None option at the bottom of the scrollable worksheet window. Clicking the None option removes all formatting from the selected range. You also can click the Options button near the upper-right of the dialog box to display a Formats to apply section at the bottom of the dialog box. In this section you can clear check boxes for formatting elements that you did not want to appear in the AutoFormat option chosen in the scrollable window. For example, clearing the Font check box removes bold and/or italic formatting and returns the font to its default style.

Figure 3-28 AutoFormat dialog box, Simple style selected

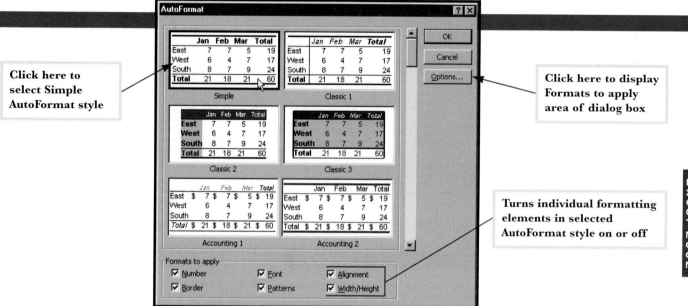

Click here to select Simple AutoFormat style

Click here to display Formats to apply area of dialog box

Turns individual formatting elements in selected AutoFormat style on or off

Figure 3-29 Simple style applied to worksheet documentation and data

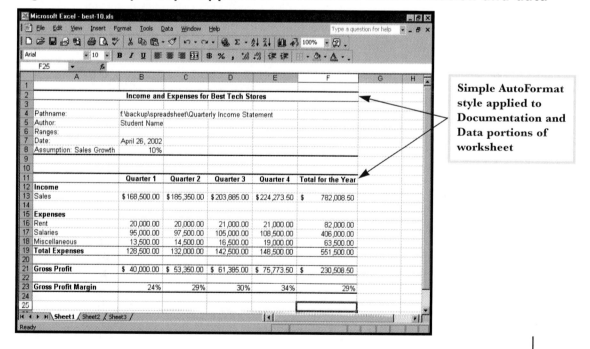

Simple AutoFormat style applied to Documentation and Data portions of worksheet

Practice

To practice AutoFormatting a worksheet, follow the instructions on the Practice3-10 Sheet tab of the practice file exprac3.xls. Save three files as directed in the Practice tab instructions, and close the files.

shortcuts

Function	Button/Mouse	Menu	Keyboard
Merge cells		Click Format, click Cells, click Alignment, then turn on Merge cells check box	
Split cells		Click Format, click Cells, click Alignment, then turn off Merge cells check box	
Copy format from selected cells to destination cells	🖌		
Merge cells and center contents of merged cells	▦	Click Format, click Cells, click Alignment, click Horizontal text box, click Center, turn on Merge cells check box	
Align cell contents to left	▤	Click Format, click Cells, click Alignment, click Horizontal text box, click Left	
Center cell contents	▤	Click Format, click Cells, click Alignment, click Horizontal text box, click Center	
Align cell contents to right	▤	Click Format, click Cells, click Alignment, click click Horizontal text box, click Right	
Bold cell contents	**B**	Click Format, click Cells, click Font, click Bold	[Ctrl]+[B]
Italicize cell contents	*I*	Click Format, click Cells, click Font, click Italic	[Ctrl]+[I]
Underline cell contents	U̲	Click Format, click Cells, click Font, click Underline	[Ctrl]+[U]
Select font color of selected text or data	A▾	Click Format, click Cells, click Font, click Color	
Decrease or increase indent	🔳 🔳	Click Format, click Cells, click Alignment tab, click Horizontal	
Apply Comma Style	,	Click Format, click Style, click Style name, click Comma	[Ctrl]+[Shift]+[!]
Apply Currency Style	$	Click Format, click Style, click Style name, click Currency	[Ctrl]+[Shift]+[$]
Apply Percent Style	%	Click Format, click Style, click Style name, click Percent	[Ctrl]+[Shift]+[%]
Increase or decrease decimal places	⊹.00 .00⊹	Click Format, click Cells, click Number tab	
Select fill color of selected cell	🖍▾	Click Format, click Cells, click Patterns, click Color	
Select all	▢	Click Edit, click Select All	[Ctrl]+[A]

A. Identify Key Features

Name the items indicated by callouts in Figure 3-30.

1. _____
2. _____
3. _____
4. _____
5. _____
6. _____
7. _____
8. _____
9. _____

Figure 3-30 Formatting features

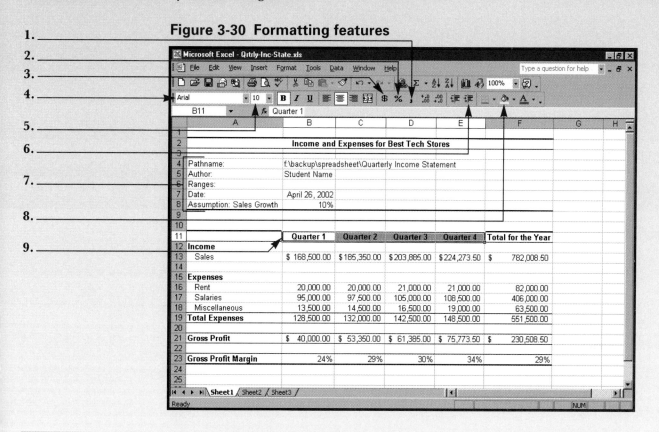

B. Select the Best Answer

10. Adds a dollar sign and two decimal places signifying cents

11. Combines multiple cells into one cell

12. Contains a tab with options for changing font, font style, and font size

13. Enables you to add a predetermined set of formatting options to a worksheet

14. Contains the Bold, Italic, and Underline buttons

15. A group of two or more cells, usually adjacent and containing related data

16. A blank cell at the bottom, but within, a defined cell range

17. A word representing a cell, cell range, formula, or constant

a. Merged cells check box

b. AutoFormat

c. Range name

d. Currency style

e. Formatting toolbar

f. Cell range

g. Format cells dialog box

h. Dummy row

quiz (continued)

C. Complete the Statement

18. All of the following are effects available on the Font tab of the Format Cells dialog box **except**:

    a. Strikethrough

    b. Strikescript

    c. Superscript

    d. Subscript

19. Excel expresses a range address as follows:

    a. B9/E9

    b. B9:E9

    c. B9;E9

    d. B9-E9

20. The Formatting toolbar offers all of the following formatting buttons except:

    a. Currency Style

    b. Comma Style

    c. Fraction Style

    d. Percent Style

21. A range name must not contain:

    a. Letters

    b. Numbers

    c. Uppercase letters

    d. Spaces

22. The standard width of an Excel worksheet column is:

    a. 8.43 characters

    b. 10.00 characters

    c. 4.83 characters

    d. 72 characters

23. Row height is measured in:

    a. Points

    b. Inches

    c. Pixels

    d. Characters

24. You can do all of the following from the Insert menu **except**:

    a. Define and name a cell range

    b. Insert a blank column

    c. Insert a blank row

    d. Access the AutoFormat command

25. Classic 2 and Colorful 2 are:

    a. Formula functions

    b. AutoFormat Styles

    c. Acceptable cell range name formats

    d. Cell values

26. When you merge two or more cells, the cell reference becomes:

    a. The last cell you typed in among the merged cells

    b. The upper-left cell of the component cells

    c. The lower-right cell of the component cells

    d. The cell you specified in the Merged cells text box

27. All of the following are examples of series data that you can enter on a worksheet **except**:

    a. Linear

    b. Currency

    c. Growth

    d. AutoFill

interactivity

Build Your Skills

1. Modify rows and columns in a worksheet:

   a. Open Student File exskills3.xls and save it as NDS Income Statement.xls. Insert one blank row above row 3. Insert two blank rows above the new row 8.

   b. In cell A8, type Current Date:. In cell B8, type today's date. Using the Format Cells dialog box, format the date using the 3/14/2001 format.

   c. In cell F10, type the label Total for the Year. Drag the right edge of the gray heading for column F until the ScreenTip reads Width: 17:00 (124 pixels). Hide rows 25 and 26, and resave the worksheet.

2. Format cell labels:

   a. Merge and center cells A2:F2 into one cell. Format the title with 14-point Tahoma font, bold and italicized. Bold the text in cells A4:A23.

   b. Double-click the right edge of column A to autofit it to the width of cell A7. Indent the text once in cell A12 and in cells A16:A20.

   c. Bold, underline, and center the text in cells B10:F10. (Do **not** merge and center the text.) Resave the worksheet.

3. Format cell values and name cell ranges:

   a. Select cells B6:B7, and format them with the Percent Style button. Select cells B11:F23, and format them with the Currency Style button.

   b. Select cells B12:F21, and use the Format Cells dialog box to delete the dollar sign symbol.

   c. Using either the Name box to the left of the Formula bar or the Define Name dialog box, name cell range B13:E13 as Gross_Profit. Name cell range B21:E21 as Total_Expenses. Name cell range B23:E23 as PreTax_Income. Resave the worksheet.

4. Apply advanced formatting to the worksheet:

   a. Click cell B10, and type Quarter 1. Using the Autofill technique, drag into cell E10 to change the remaining labels to Quarter 2, Quarter 3, and Quarter 4. (If a Smart Tag appears above cell F11, ignore it, as the next Step will clear it.)

   b. Select cell A2, cells B10:F10, and cells B23:F23. Using the Format Cells dialog box, apply a solid Indigo border around the selected cells. Also apply a Light Blue background fill and a 12.5% Gray pattern.

   c. Click the Select All button (the gray square to the left of the column A heading), click Edit, click Clear, and click Formats.

   d. Select the cells A2:F8. Using AutoFormat, select the Accounting 2 style, click Options, clear the Number check box, and press [Enter]. Remerge and center cells A2:F2.

   e. Reapply the Percent format to cells B6:B7, and reapply a Date format of your own choosing to cell B8.

   f. Select cells A10:F23. Using AutoFormat, select the Accounting 2 style, and press [Enter]. Unbold cell A15. Resave your worksheet.

interactivity (continued)

Problem Solving Exercises

1. Use the skills you have learned about spreadsheet design to help track your progress toward your diploma. Create an Excel worksheet with three parts: (1) List the general graduation requirements for your major (e.g., minimum credits for graduation, minimum credits in your major, credits required for minors, and so on). (2) List your courses already taken, current courses, and remaining courses needed for graduation. Group all of the courses by semester or quarter, depending on your school's calendar. Enter grades for only your completed courses. Calculate your semester-by-semester Grade Point Average and your cumulative GPA. Save the file as GPA Requirements.xls.

2. Design a worksheet to track stocks that you might invest in. Use a newspaper or the Internet (www.nasdaq.com, for example) to find names and stock data on nine companies (e.g., car companies, chain stores, and so on). In a Company Name column, enter their names alphabetically. In an Initials column, enter their stock initials. In a Week 1 column, enter their closing prices as of the week before last. In a Week 2 column, enter closing prices for last week. In a Price Change column, use a formula to calculate their change in price from Week 1 to Week 2. In a Percent Change column, use a formula to calculate the percent of change between the weeks, formatting it with Percent Style. In a Totals row, use the SUM formula to calculate totals for all nine stocks. Format the Week 1, Week 2, and Price Change columns with Currency Style. Merge and center the main title. Bold and center the heading labels. Format appropriate titles and headings with a solid line border and a light background color. Save the worksheet as Personal Stocks-1.xls.

3. Open Student File exproblem3-1.xls, which resembles the file, Personal Stocks-1.xls. Save exproblem3-1.xls as Personal Stocks-2.xls. Add a tenth company to the chart, filling in all its columns with appropriate data and formatting. Between the Initials and Week 1 columns, insert a column entitled No. of Shares; enter a quantity of shares between 5 and 10. After the rightmost column, add a column entitled Profit/(Loss); use a formula and AutoFill to calculate profit or loss based on No. of Shares times Price Change. Format the two new columns with appropriate formatting. Apply Names to the cell ranges in each column except the first. When applying names, include just the ten rows that correspond with the companies. After inserting the tenth company, inserting and formatting the two columns, calculating formulas, and naming cell ranges, use AutoFormat to reformat the worksheet to look organized, readable, and attractive.

4. Reproduce the worksheet in Figure 3-31 as closely as possible. Delete column C, add two additional columns to the right, use AutoFill to retitle the appropriate columns as January through June, and add additional data to the May and the June columns. Format the heading labels to be readable and attractive. Format the data below the headings properly so the data represents dollars and cents. Save the worksheet as Format Practice.xls. Print the worksheet on one page.

Figure 3-31 Formatting.xls

	B	C	D	E	F	G
1			Quarter 1	Quarter 2	Quarter 3	Quarter 4
2 1	Charles Bailey		850.3	900.55	910.45	950.74
3 2	Wilma Davidson		874.55	850.23	860.78	880.45
4 3	Alfred Lum		982.88	950.55	960.89	980.56
5 4	Roberto Martines		974.12	971.24	981.35	1000.23
6 5	Andrew Opperman		850.66	840.75	855.56	890.15
7 6	Libby Seasons		789.23	781.44	799.23	851.59
8 7	Samuel Tanaka		987.32	977.3	988.77	1005.26

Inserting Objects and Charts

The labels and values that you enter into a worksheet provide the main information that people need in such a document. However, objects may be more informative than pure data or illustrate your data further. Inserting these objects can break up the monotony of row after row of numbers and enable you to highlight or explain aspects of your worksheet that might otherwise go unnoticed.

You can insert a number of objects into your worksheet for the purpose of annotating specific information. These objects include text boxes, shapes such as arrows and connectors, and comments. Text boxes can be any size, but will obscure the portions of the worksheet behind them. Comments resemble text boxes, but you can hide them from view. Additionally, you can format and manipulate all graphics in many ways.

One effective way to enhance a worksheet visually is to add a chart. Excel's Chart Wizard guides you through the process of creating a graphical representation of a data series that you select from your worksheet. After creating a chart, you can move, resize, and format it. You can change the type of chart and its characteristics after creating it. You also can customize individual elements of the chart to provide emphasis or greater clarity. And once you have created, formatted, and customized the chart, you can print it along with its related data.

Lesson Goal:

Strengthen a worksheet by inserting graphics and creating a chart using the Chart Wizard. Use some of Excel's advanced printing features to print a new copy of the worksheet.

skills

- ⚡ **Inserting Text Objects**
- ⚡ **Enhancing Graphics**
- ⚡ **Adding and Editing Comments**
- ⚡ **Understanding Excel Charts**
- ⚡ **Creating a Chart**
- ⚡ **Moving and Resizing a Chart**
- ⚡ **Formatting a Chart**
- ⚡ **Changing a Chart's Type**
- ⚡ **Using Advanced Printing Features**

skill   Inserting Text Objects

concept

Lessons 1 to 3 show how to insert text into worksheet cells by clicking cells and typing. But you also can insert text into a worksheet within a text box. Such boxes enable you to add words and sentences of any size and appearance outside the constraints of a worksheet cell. A text box is an independent object, like a sticky note, that you can place anywhere on the worksheet. You also can move, resize, and reformat text boxes. And since text boxes are independent of cells, such boxes can reference worksheet data without affecting that data.

do it !

Insert a text box into a worksheet to emphasize the growth in Quarter 4 sales.

1. Open Student File exdoit4-1.xls and save it as Text Boxes.xls.

2. Click View, click Toolbars, then click Drawing to display the Drawing toolbar. If necessary, dock the toolbar at the bottom of the program window.

3. Click the Text Box button 📰 on the Drawing toolbar. When you move your mouse pointer onto the worksheet, the pointer will change to the text cursor [↓] to indicate that you can create a text box.

4. Scroll as needed to make cell E9 appear in the worksheet window. Position the pointer just below the purple line where you want the top-left corner of the text box to appear. While holding down the mouse button, drag to the lower-right corner of cell E10 so the text box will be one cell wide and two cells tall (see Figure 4-1). ⬤ When you release the mouse button, the box borders will become dotted and eight small circles—called sizing handles—will appear at the corners and at the midpoints of the four box sides. A blinking insertion point will appear in the text box.

5. With the insertion point in the upper-left corner of the text box, type Up 33% from Quarter 1. When text reaches the right edge of the text box, it automatically will wrap to the second line. Click outside the text box to cancel the selection. Your worksheet should look like Figure 4-2.

6. Save and close your worksheet with the changes you have made.

more

The primary advantage of using text boxes is their flexibility. You easily can move, resize, or reformat text boxes without affecting the appearance or content of any other part of the worksheet. When text is being entered, a text box acts as a small word processing window. If the text box is not large enough to fit a word or phrase on one line, the text will wrap and continue onto the next line. If the text box is too small to accommodate all the text as you enter it, then the text will scroll upward, without changing the size or location of the box, to allow you to enter more text. You then must enlarge a text box manually to view all of the text it contains. You can do this by dragging a handle in the desired direction to expand the box. If you remove text from a text box, you can drag the proper sizing handle inward to shrink the box.

Once you create a text box, it is not fixed in place. You can move it anywhere on the worksheet. To move a text box to another part of the worksheet, click the frame of a selected text box—not a sizing handle—to select its frame, then drag the text box to the desired location. To learn how to reformat a text box, consult the next Skill.

Figure 4-1 Set Title in Black

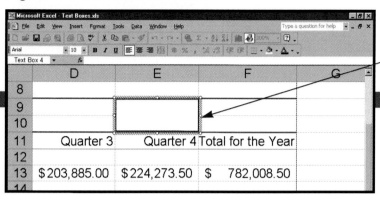

New text box is one cell wide and two cells tall; border is dotted and displays eight sizing handles

Figure 4-2 Worksheet's appearance after adding text to text box

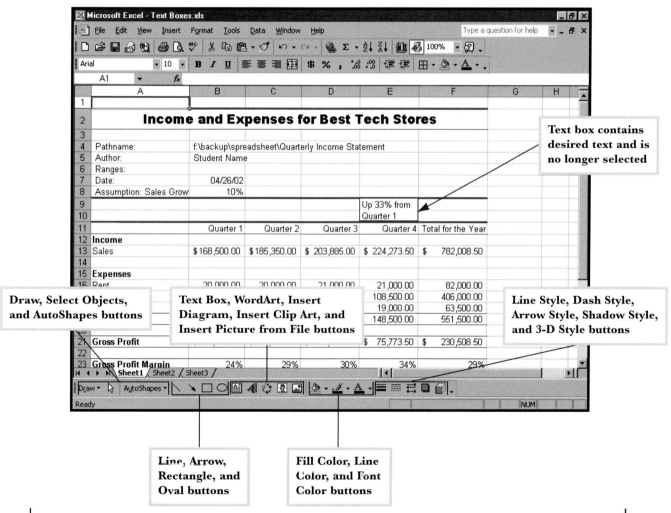

Text box contains desired text and is no longer selected

Draw, Select Objects, and AutoShapes buttons

Text Box, WordArt, Insert Diagram, Insert Clip Art, and Insert Picture from File buttons

Line Style, Dash Style, Arrow Style, Shadow Style, and 3-D Style buttons

Line, Arrow, Rectangle, and Oval buttons

Fill Color, Line Color, and Font Color buttons

Practice

To practice inserting text boxes, follow the instructions on the Practice4-1 Sheet tab of the practice file exprac4.xls. Save changes as myexprac4-1.xls and close the file.

skill   Enhancing Graphics

concept

After you insert graphics such as text boxes, pictures, arrows, and the like, you can edit their appearance to make them more emphatic or attractive. Excel users might emphasize a text box or other graphic to call attention to an important part of a worksheet. By making your graphics more attractive, people are more likely to pay attention to them, especially if they are part of a color presentation, Internet site, and so on.

do it !

Add a callout arrow, add color to a text box, and bold the font so it stands out in the box.

1. Open Student File exdoit4-2.xls and save it as Enhancing Graphics.xls.

2. Click the Arrow button ◥ on the Drawing toolbar. The mouse pointer will appear as a thin cross [+] when it is over the worksheet.

3. In the text box that covers cells E9:E10, position the pointer halfway between the number 1 and the right edge of the text box. While holding down the mouse button, drag to the top center edge of cell E13, which contains the Sales value for Quarter 4. Release the mouse button. The line that you have drawn will be fixed, and an arrowhead will appear at the lower end of the line.

4. Click the text box to select it. Its frame will become a thick, hatched line. Click the frame of the text box, but not a sizing handle. The frame will change from the thick hatched line to a dotted border.

5. On the Drawing toolbar, click the arrow on the Fill Color button ◨▾ to open the Fill Color palette. Click the Pale Blue square in the bottom row, sixth column, to select it. The background of the text box will change to match the selected square (see Figure 4-3).

6. Click the arrow that you drew in Step 3 to select it. A sizing handle will appear at each end of the arrow to indicate its selection. Click the arrow on the Line Color button ◢▾ to open the Line Color palette. Click the Dark Blue square in the first row, sixth column, to select it. The arrow will change color to match the selected square (see Figure 4-4).

7. Click once in the text box, then select all of the text inside it. Click the Bold button **B** to bold the text. Click outside of the text box.

8. Compare the text box arrow, the text box shading, and the bold font with Figure 4-5. If necessary, redo the Steps above to correct any errors.

9. Save and close the worksheet with the changes you have made.

more

Excel's Format menu is context sensitive; that is, its content changes based on what worksheet item is selected. When a cell is active, the Format menu contains commands for altering a cell. When an AutoShape is active, the menu contains commands related to AutoShapes. Objects inserted into an Excel document—such as lines and Clip Art—all have their own formatting dialog boxes with tabs relating to the selected object.

The Format Text Box command, available on the Format menu when a text box is active, opens the Format Text Box dialog box (see Figure 4-6). This dialog box contains eight tabs with options for altering many aspects of a text box. While many controls in the dialog box have corresponding toolbar buttons, the dialog box permits more precise and comprehensive control over item aspects such as text box size, internal margins of a text box, and text orientation within a text box.

Figure 4-3 Fill Color palette

Figure 4-4 Line Color palette

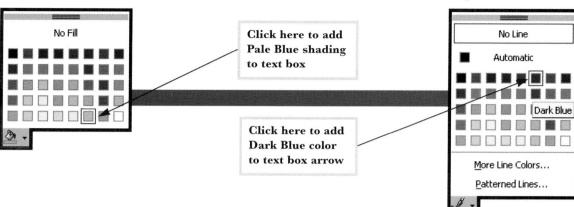

Click here to add
Pale Blue shading
to text box

Click here to add
Dark Blue color
to text box arrow

Figure 4-5 Worksheet with enhanced graphic

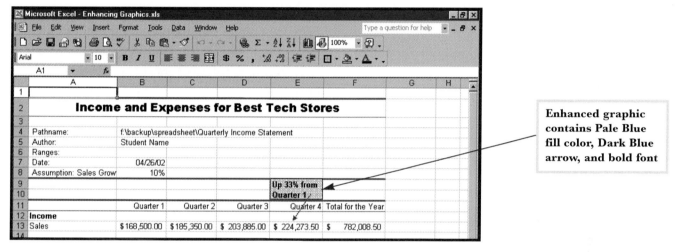

Enhanced graphic
contains Pale Blue
fill color, Dark Blue
arrow, and bold font

Figure 4-6 Font tab of Format Text Box dialog box

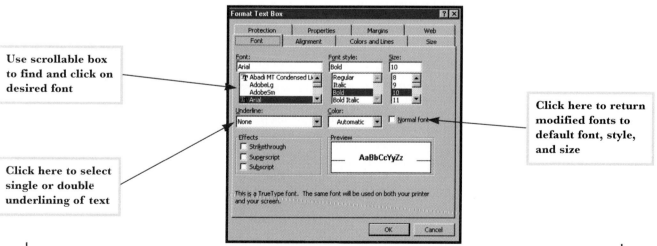

Use scrollable box
to find and click on
desired font

Click here to return
modified fonts to
default font, style,
and size

Click here to select
single or double
underlining of text

Practice

To practice enhancing graphics, follow the instructions on the Practice4-2 Sheet tab of the practice file exprac4.xls. Save changes as myexprac4-2.xls and close the file.

skill Adding and Editing Comments

concept

A comment is an electronic note that you can attach to a cell. A comment does not display unless the mouse pointer hovers over a cell containing that comment. Comments help to document information or provide clarifying or explanatory notes. If several people access a worksheet at school, at work, or on the Internet, comments can be used to share information without cluttering the worksheet with extra text. If the worksheet users place their mouse pointers over the proper cell, however, the comment then will appear to provide more information.

do it !

Insert a comment to list the names of cell ranges on a worksheet.

1. Open Student File exdoit4-3.xls and save it as Comments.xls. Click cell B5 to make it active. Type the name Kyle Samuel in the cell and press [Enter]. Click the cell again.

2. Click Insert, then click Comment. An active text box with the name of the program's designated user and an insertion point will appear next to the selected cell. The text box will have an arrow pointing to the cell that it references, and a small red triangle will appear in the upper-right corner of the cell to indicate that it contains a comment.

3. Select the contents of the cell by dragging the I-beam over the text in the box. Type Kyle Samuel: and press [Enter] (see Figure 4-7). Notice that the name that first appeared in the comment box appears in the Status bar at the bottom of the program window.

4. Type the following range names, exactly as listed, pressing [Enter] after each one: Gross Profit, Gross Profit Margin, Miscellaneous, Quarter 1, Quarter 2, Quarter 3, Rent, Salaries, Sales, and Total Expenses.

5. Drag down the midpoint sizing handle at the bottom edge of the comment box until you can see the words Total Expenses at the bottom of the box. Release the mouse button (see Figure 4-8).

6. Click elsewhere on the worksheet to cancel the selection of cell B5 and to hide the comment. Position the mouse pointer over cell B5 to display the comment. Notice that the words Quarter 4 are missing from the list of cell range names.

7. Click cell B5 to select it. Remember that, under this condition, the comment will display only as long as the mouse pointer is over the cell. Click Insert, then click Edit Comment. Because you have clicked the editing command, the comment will display and stay visible even if you move the mouse pointer elsewhere without clicking in a cell.

8. Click at the end of the words Quarter 3 and press [Enter]. Type the words Quarter 4 to add them to the comment box (see Figure 4-9). Click in a cell other than B5 to move the mouse pointer out of the comment box and to close it.

9. Save and close the worksheet with the changes you have made.

more Like cells and text boxes, comment boxes and the text they contain can be formatted. To format a comment box, right-click the cell with the comment to display a shortcut menu containing the Edit Comment command used in Step 7 and a Delete Comment and a Show Comment command. If you click Edit Comment, the insertion point appears in the comment box, and you can start typing where needed as in Step 9. The comment box also will have hatch marks around it, indicating you can resize or move the box. (Wherever you move the comment box, an arrow will run from the comment to its parent cell). If you click Show Comment, you need to click the comment box before formatting. Double-clicking the comment box border opens the Format Comment dialog box with eight tabs containing options for formatting fonts, alignment, text direction, margins, and so on. Click View, click Toolbars, then click Reviewing to open the Reviewing toolbar containing commands for displaying and navigating among comments (see Figure 4-10).

Figure 4-7 Comment box with Kyle Samuel's name

Click Insert to access Comment commands

Small red triangle indicates cell containing comment

Hatchmarks indicate text within box is available for typing or editing

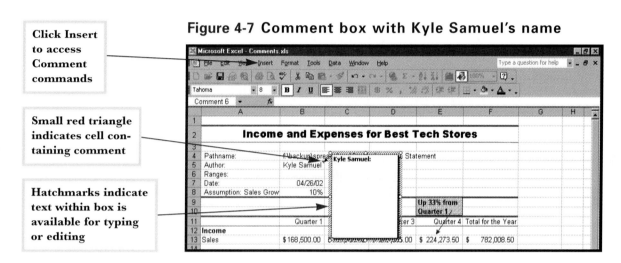

Figure 4-8 Comment box with list of cell range names

Kyle Samuel:
Gross Profit
Gross Profit Margin
Miscellaneous
Quarter 1
Quarter 2
Quarter 3
Rent
Salaries
Sales
Total Expenses

Figure 4-9 Comment box with revised list of cell range names

Kyle Samuel:
Gross Profit
Gross Profit Margin
Miscellaneous
Quarter 1
Quarter 2
Quarter 3
Quarter 4
Rent
Salaries
Sales
Total Expenses

Figure 4-10 Reviewing toolbar

Edit Comment, Previous Comment, and Next Comment buttons

Show Comment, Show All Comments, and Delete Comment buttons

Create MS Outlook Task, Update File, and Send to Mail Recipient buttons

Practice

To practice adding and editing comments, follow the instructions on the Practice4-3 Sheet tab of the practice file exprac4.xls. Save changes as myexprac4-3.xls and close the file.

skill | Understanding Excel Charts

concept

In Excel you can create charts in worksheets to provide greater visual appeal and to help you quickly understand complicated data. For example, a chart based on an income statement such as Best Tech's can portray several rows and columns of worksheet numbers in just one graphic. This graphic can help you determine if your income is rising or falling, decide whether you are controlling expenses quarter by quarter, or display the relation between overall sales and gross profits. Whatever a chart represents, be sure it helps you understand your data more readily while portraying the data simply and attractively.

do it !

Creating Charts

Before creating a chart, you must enter data for it on a worksheet. You then must select that data and use the Chart Wizard, a series of dialog boxes that take you through four steps: (1) choosing a chart type, (2) deciding on source data, (3) selecting chart options, and (4) choosing a chart location. Alternately, you can use the Chart toolbar to create a chart and then format it. Whether you use the Chart Wizard or Chart toolbar, you can embed a chart on its related worksheets or put it on another sheet. You also can publish charts to the Web.

How Charts Represent Worksheet Data

As already noted, worksheet data provide the basis for a chart's data segments, whether they are columns, pie wedges, dots on a line, or so on. Because worksheet data and their related charts are linked, the chart automatically updates whenever you change the worksheet data on which the chart is based. A finished chart (see examples on the next page) should have all of the following elements, unless they are not appropriate to the type of chart you have chosen:

- **Data markers** – are columns, lines, pie wedges, or so on representing a data point, or single value, from a related worksheet; markers with the same color represent a data series.

- **Major gridlines** – are horizontal and/or vertical backdrops for chart values; for example, in a chart with vertical columns, horizontal gridlines will mark major value levels; larger charts also can have minor gridlines.

- **Category axis names** – are labels on the horizontal (X) or vertical (Y) axes identifying the individual items you are charting; these names come from row or column headings in a related worksheet.

- **Chart data series names** – are titles identifying the larger class or group that the individual chart items fall into; these names can come from columns or rows on a related worksheet, or you can add them in the Chart Wizard; data series names appear in the Legend.

If you rest your mouse pointer over a chart element, a ScreenTip will appear that contains the name of that element.

Embedded Charts and Chart Sheets

Embedded charts—are graphic objects saved as part of the worksheet from which you created the charts. Use these charts whenever you want to display or print one or more charts beside its related worksheet.

Chart sheets—are separate sheets in a workbook with their own sheets and, usually, sheet names. Use these sheets when you need to reserve the related worksheet for data itself and/or when the chart itself is too large or complicated for its related worksheet. With the chart on its own chart sheet, you also can view or edit it separately from the related worksheet.

Figure 4-11 Sample Column Chart

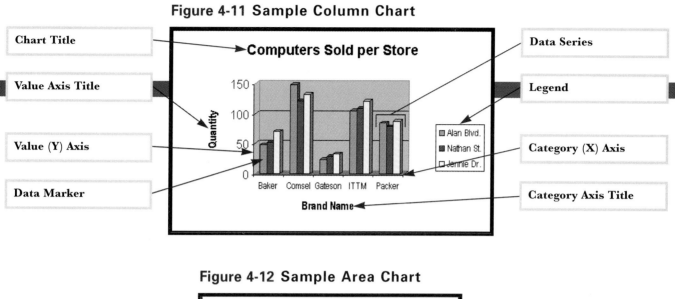

Chart Title

Value Axis Title

Value (Y) Axis

Data Marker

Data Series

Legend

Category (X) Axis

Category Axis Title

Figure 4-12 Sample Area Chart

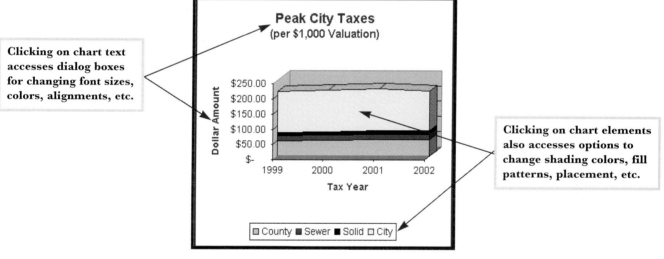

Clicking on chart text accesses dialog boxes for changing font sizes, colors, alignments, etc.

Clicking on chart elements also accesses options to change shading colors, fill patterns, placement, etc.

Figure 4-13 Sample Line Chart

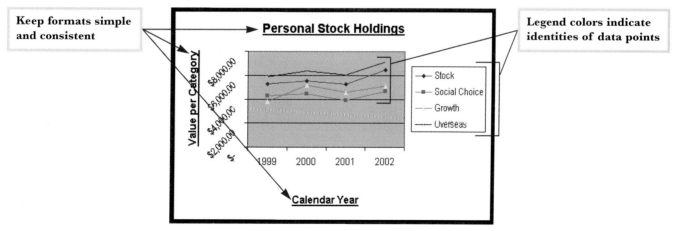

Keep formats simple and consistent

Legend colors indicate identities of data points

skill

Creating a Chart

MOUS Skill

concept

Charts are graphics that represent values and their relationships. Using charts, you quickly can identify trends in data and see contrasts among values. Excel enables you to portray data easily using a variety of two- and three-dimensional chart styles. These styles give data immediate meaning, unlike data in its raw form, which generally requires studying.

do it !

Use a pie chart to show values for Rent, Salaries, and Miscellaneous Expenses as a percentage of total yearly expenses.

1. Open Student File exdoit4-5.xls and save it as Create Chart.xls. Select cell range F16:F18 to choose the values desired for a new chart.

2. Click the Chart Wizard button on the Standard toolbar. The Chart Wizard dialog box opens with the Column chart type selected. If the Office Assistant appears, close it by clicking the No, I do not want help now option, as you do not need the Assistant for this Skill.

3. In the Chart type list box, click Pie. The Chart subtypes will change to show different types of pie charts (see Figure 4-14). The basic pie chart sub-type is selected by default.

4. Click ⎡ Next > ⎤. The Wizard will advance to Step 2 with a two-dimensional pie chart representing the selected data displayed. If you had not already selected cells, you could enter which cells to include in your chart by entering that data in the Data range text box.

5. Click the Series tab to bring it forward in the dialog box. Be sure that the Values text box reads =Sheet1!$F$16:$F$18 (see Figure 4-15).

6. Click the Category Labels text box to activate it. A flashing insertion point will appear in the text box so you can name the categories for your chart.

7. Click the Collapse Dialog button at the right end of the Category Labels text box. The dialog box will shrink so only the Category Labels text box is shown. Collapsing the dialog box allows you to view more of the worksheet so you easily can select the cells to be inserted as the labels for your chart's categories. If necessary, drag the text box to the right of Column B and scroll up slightly so rows 16–18 appear near the top of the worksheet.

8. Select cell range A16:A18. A moving border will surround the selected range, a ScreenTip will display the size of the selection, and the range will appear in the collapsed dialog box (see Figure 4-16).

9. Click the Expand Dialog button at the right end of the collapsed dialog box to bring the full dialog box back into view. Be sure that the Category Labels text box reads =Sheet1!$A$16:$A$18 (see Figure 4-17).

(continued on EX 4.12)

Figure 4-14 Chart Wizard—Step 1

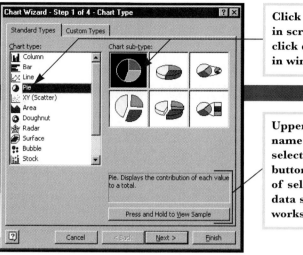

Click main chart type in scrollable box; click desired sub-type in window to right

Upper area displays name and use of selected chart; click button to view sample of selected chart with data selected from worksheet

Figure 4-15 Series tab of Step 2

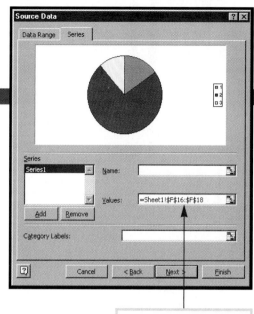

Displays cell range of series you selected in related worksheet

Figure 4-16 Collapsed dialog box

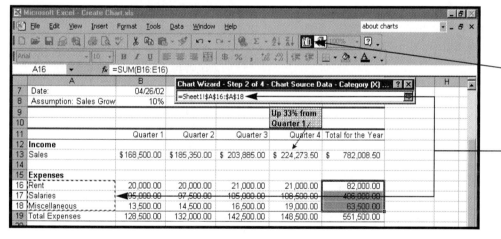

Chart Wizard button

Collapsed dialog box displays cell range selected in animated area at left

Figure 4-17 Re-enlarged Chart Wizard

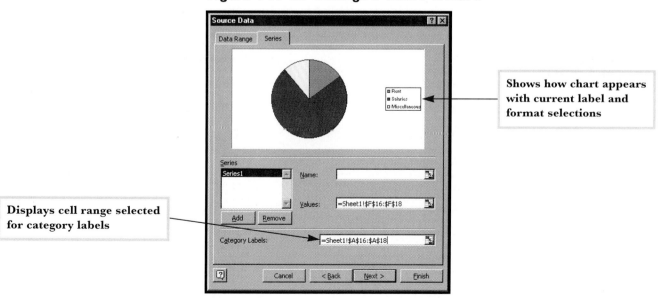

Shows how chart appears with current label and format selections

Displays cell range selected for category labels

skill Creating a Chart (cont'd)

do it !

10. Click the Next button [Next >]. Step 3 of the Chart Wizard will appear. Click the Chart title text box, then type Breakdown of Expenses. The title you have entered will appear in the preview area in the right side of the dialog box. The other text boxes are grayed out since they do not apply to the selected chart type.

11. Click the Legend tab to bring it forward in the dialog box. A check mark appears by default in the Show legend check box. Click the Show legend check box to deselect this option, as you will label the chart later.

12. Click the Data Labels tab to bring it forward. In the Label Contains section, put check marks in the Category Name check box and the Percentages check box. Labels and percentages will appear in the preview area at the right side of the dialog box (see Figure 4-18).

13. Click the Next button [Next >]. Step 4 of the Chart Wizard will appear. The As object in option button is selected by default, indicating that the chart would appear in the current worksheet as opposed to a new one if you closed the dialog box now (see Figure 4-19).

14. Click the Finish button [Finish]. The Chart Wizard dialog box will close, your chart will display in the center of your worksheet, and the Chart toolbar will appear in the Excel window (see Figure 4-20).

15. Save and close your workbook with the changes you have made.

more

When you select a chart, the Chart menu replaces the Data menu. The first four commands on the Chart menu open dialog boxes that resemble the steps of the Chart Wizard. These commands enable you to alter any of the characteristics of the chart without having to recreate it in the Chart Wizard. The Add Data command lets you append the ranges that are displayed.

Table 4-1 describes some common chart types and gives examples of how to you might use them.

Table 4-1

Chart Type		Description	Example
Area		Emphasizes magnitude of change over time	Increases from tax sources
Bar		Similar to column chart, but emphasizes X value	Individual sales performance
Column		Shows how data changes over time	Quarterly income projections
Line		Shows trends in data at equal intervals	Monthly gross and net sales
Pie		Shows relation of individual parts to sum of parts	Budgets, country exports
Stock		Indicates various values of stocks	Low, high, and closing prices

Figure 4-18 Data Labels tab of Step 3

Turns labels of
selected chart ele-
ments on or off;
options selected
here replace
Legend deleted
on previous tab of
dialog box

Click Titles tab to apply
chart title and other
titles appropriate for
selected chart; click
Legend tab to display,
format, or hide Legend

Turns relevant color
boxes and leader
lines from labels to
pie wedges on or off

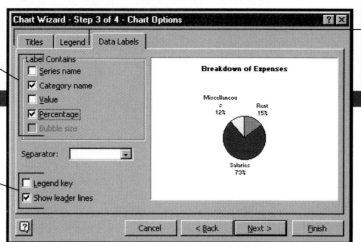

Figure 4-19 Chart Wizard—Step 4

Click option button and
type name of new work-
sheet for chart to appear on

Accept this selection and
click [Finish] button to
place chart on its relat-
ed worksheet

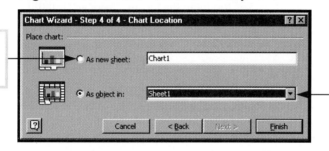

Figure 4-20 Chart displayed as object in worksheet

After closing Chart Wizard,
chart appears in center of
selected worksheet

With chart selected,
Chart toolbar appears
in worksheet window

Chart Values chosen in
Step 1; Type in Step 4,
Category Labels in Step 8,
and Worksheet in Step 13

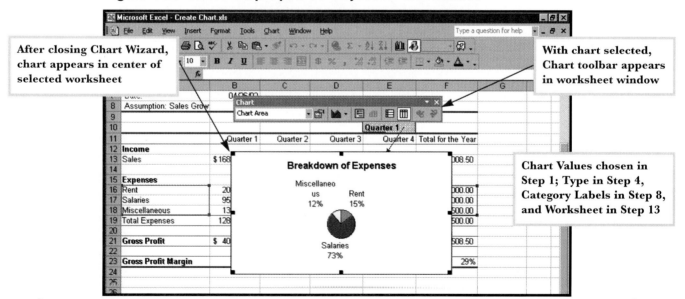

Practice

To practice creating a chart, follow the instructions on the Practice4-5 Sheet tab of the practice file
exprac4.xls. Save changes as myexprac4-5.xls and close the file.

skill | Moving and Resizing a Chart

concept

Once you have created a chart, you can change its location and size on the worksheet so the chart has an attractive shape and does not obstruct your view of the data in the worksheet itself. Depending on the size and orientation of your page, you generally would place the chart to the right or below the worksheet. With either of these locations, the data remains dominant, but the chart still adds important information to the overall presentation.

do it !

Move the chart below the main data of the worksheet and then resize it so its boundaries match those of existing rows and columns.

1. Open Student File exdoit4-6.xls and save it as Move Chart.xls.

2. Click once on the chart. Eight small black sizing handles appear at the corners and at the midpoints of the edges of the chart. Hold down the [Alt] key, and drag the chart down until the upper-left corner of the chart is even with the upper-left corner of cell B25 (see Figure 4-21). Release [Alt]. As you move the mouse, the mouse pointer will change to the movement pointer [✛], and a dotted border will indicate where the chart will appear when the mouse button is released. The worksheet will scroll upward whenever the mouse pointer is dragged below the document window.

3. If necessary, scroll down until the entire chart appears in the document window. Hold down the [Alt] key and drag the midpoint sizing handle of the right edge of the chart so the right edge of the chart is on the border between columns E and F. Release [Alt] (see Figure 4-22).

4. Hold down the [Alt] key and drag the midpoint sizing handle of the bottom edge of the chart to the boundary between rows 39 and 40 (see Figure 4-23). Release [Alt].

5. Save and close your workbook with the changes you have made.

more

Table 4-2 below summarizes different techniques you can use to move and resize charts and other objects:

Table 4-2

Action	To
Press [Shift] while dragging chart	Restrict a chart's movement to only the horizontal or vertical
Press [Ctrl] while dragging chart	Copy the chart to another place in the worksheet
Press [Ctrl] while dragging sizing handle	Maintain a chart's center point when resizing it
Press [Shift] while dragging corner sizing handle	Restrict a chart's aspect ratio when resizing it
Press [Ctrl]+[Shift] while dragging corner sizing handle	Maintain a chart's center point and aspect ratio when resizing it
Press [Alt] while dragging chart or sizing handle	Positions chart along cell borders as you drag

Figure 4-21 Chart's location after moving below worksheet

Formatting of
Miscellaneous
will be
corrected later

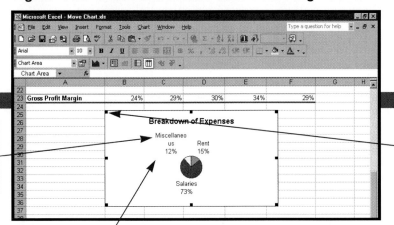

Upper-left corner of
chart matches upper-
left corner of cell B25

Figure 4-22 Chart's appearance after moving right edge

Chart elements
adjust to fit
redefined chart
area

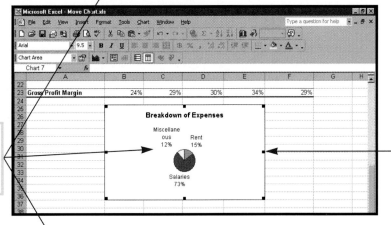

Right edge of chart
matches boundary
of columns E and F

Figure 4-23 Chart's appearance after moving bottom edge

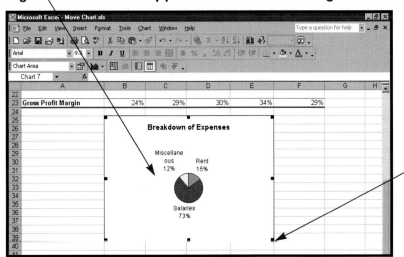

Bottom edge of chart
matches boundary of
rows 39 and 40

Practice

To practice moving and resizing a chart, follow the instructions on the Practice4-6 Sheet tab of the practice file exprac4.xls. Save changes as myexprac4-6.xls and close the file.

skill | Formatting a Chart

concept

After you create, relocate, and resize a chart, you still can alter many more of its features to make it more colorful and attractive, to highlight certain areas of the chart, to call attention to an unusual or distinctive element among several elements, and so on. Among chart features that you can change are colors, patterns, fill effects, fonts, font styles and sizes, font alignments, line widths, border effects, and so on. Before formatting an area, however, you must remember to click directly on the desired area, not a larger or smaller area of the overall chart.

do it !

Isolate the corresponding pie wedge to emphasize that a company met its goal of keeping miscellaneous expenses under 15% of total expenses. Also, change the wedge's color, format the title, and correct the formatting of a data label.

1. Open Student File exdoit4-7.xls, and save it as Format Chart.xls.

2. Click the pie in your chart to make it active. Three sizing handles will appear to indicate its selection.

3. Click the Miscellaneous pie wedge to select it. Drag the pie wedge away from the pie so the point of the wedge is even with the former border of the pie. Notice that the wedge's label moves to accommodate the wedge's new position.

4. Double-click the Miscellaneous pie wedge to open the Format Data Point dialog box. Click the Patterns tab to bring it forward. In the Area section of the tab, click the Yellow square in the third column of the bottom row. The Sample area in the lower-left region of the tab will display the newly selected color (see Figure 4-24). Click ОК to apply the selected color and to close the dialog box.

5. Double-click the chart's title, Breakdown of Expenses, to open the Format Chart Title dialog box. On the Patterns tab, click the Shadow check box to activate it (see Figure 4-25). Click ОК to apply the shadow and to close the dialog box.

6. Notice that the label Miscellaneous is spread over two lines. Double-click the word Miscellaneous to open the Format Data Labels dialog box. Click the Font tab to bring it forward. In the Font area, click Arial Narrow. In the Font style area, click Bold. In the Size area click 9. Click ОК to apply the new font and to close the dialog box. Click outside the chart to cancel the selection (see Figure 4-26).

7. Save and close the workbook with the changes you have made.

more

Double-clicking any selected chart element will open a dialog box that enables you to format and alter that element. The available tabs of the dialog box that appears will provide formatting options that are relevant to the selected item. You also may select elements and their formatting dialog boxes using the Chart toolbar (see Figure 4-27).

On the Patterns tab of the chart element formatting dialog boxes, there is a Fill Effects button that lets you apply advanced formatting options such as gradients, textures, patterns, or pictures to the selected element.

Figure 4-24 Patterns tab of Format Data Point dialog box

Figure 4-25 Patterns tab of Format Chart Point dialog box

Format Data Point
Patterns
Data Labels
Options
Border
Automatic
None
Custom
Style:
Color:
Automatic
Weight:
Shadow
Sample
Area
Automatic
None
Fill Effects...
OK
Cancel

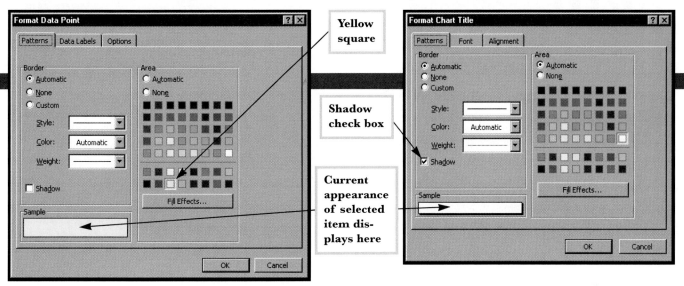

Yellow square
Shadow check box
Current appearance of selected item displays here
Format Chart Title
Patterns
Font
Alignment
Border
Automatic
None
Custom
Style:
Color:
Automatic
Weight:
Shadow
Sample
Area
Automatic
None
Fill Effects...
OK
Cancel

Figure 4-26 Formatted chart elements

All three labels have 9-point Arial, bold, format
Breakdown of Expenses
Miscellaneous
12%
Rent
15%
Salaries
73%

Figure 4-27 Chart toolbar

Chart Objects box: click here to select chart object desired for editing
Chart
Chart Area
Angle Clockwise and Angle Counterclock-wise buttons
Format Chart Area and Chart Type buttons
Legend and Data Table buttons
By Row and By Column buttons

Practice

To practice formatting a chart, follow the instructions on the Practice4-7 tab of the practice file exprac4.xls. Save changes as myexprac4-7.xls and close the file.

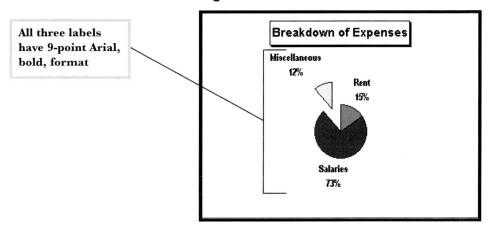

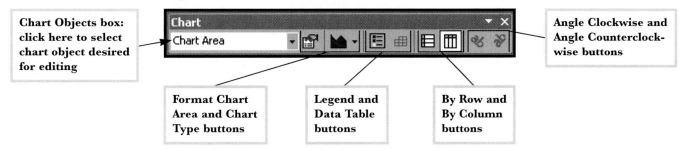

skill | Changing a Chart's Type

MOUS Skill

concept

Excel allows you to change the type of chart you already have, while referencing the same data series. For example, you could convert a column chart to a bar chart, a line chart, and so on. You also can switch between variants of the same chart type, called sub-types, to provide variety in chart style or to enhance a chart element that needs extra emphasis. Be aware that you should not change chart types if the second type would improperly represent the selected data.

do it !

Display the pie chart with a 3-D effect and increased elevation, or tilt, to the chart's bottom.

1. Open Student File exdoit4-8.xls and save it as Change Chart.xls.

2. Select the chart, click Chart on the Menu bar, then click the Chart Type command to open the Chart Type dialog box. The Standard Types tab should be in front. If it is not, click it to bring it forward, where you will see the selected chart type and available sub-types.

3. In the Chart sub-type area, click the image in the first row, second column. It will high-light, and its name—Pie with a 3-D visual effect—will appear below the Chart sub-type area (see Figure 4-28). Click OK to apply the 3-D effect and close the dialog box.

4. Click Chart, then click 3-D View to open the 3-D View dialog box. In the Elevation text box, the current elevation of 15 degrees will appear. Click the Increase Elevation arrow ⬆ three times to increase the pie's elevation to 30 degrees, as shown in Figure 4-29. The preview area of the dialog box will display the changing elevation of as you click the arrow. Click OK to apply the new elevation and to close the dialog box. Instead of clicking the Increase Elevation arrow, you could highlight the Elevation text box, then type 30. Pressing [Enter] would apply the new elevation and close the dialog box. Alternatively, you could click the Apply button Apply to see how the new eleva-tion would look, then click OK to accept it and to close the dialog box.

5. Click in cell G25, outside the chart area. Verify that your chart looks like the one in Figure 4-30. If necessary, redo the Steps above to match the appearance of the figure. Save and close the workbook with the changes you have made.

more

For most two-dimensional charts, you can change the type of chart for either a data series or for the entire chart. (Remember that a data series is a set of related data points that appear in a chart.) For most three-dimensional charts, you will change the entire chart when changing the type of chart. However, for three-dimensional bar charts and column charts, you can change a data series to either a cone, cylinder, or pyramid type of chart. For bubble charts you can change only the entire chart type.

To change a type of chart in which you can change either the entire chart or just a data series, you must remember to click directly on the desired area, not a larger or smaller area than you wish to change. Therefore, to change the entire chart, you must click on the overall chart. But to change just a data series, you must click on only the desired data series. After clicking on only the desired data series, you also must put a check mark in the Apply to selection check box in the Options area on the Standard Types tab of the Chart Type dialog box.

Suppose that you want to change a three-dimensional bar data series or column data series to the cone, cylinder, or pyramid type of chart. In this case, click Chart, click Chart Type to open the Chart Type dialog box, and click the Standard Types tab to bring it to the front of the dialog box. Then click either the Cone, Cylinder, or Pyramid option in the Chart type box and add a check box to the Apply to selection check box.

Figure 4-28 Chart Type dialog box with 3-D pie effect selected

Option becomes unavailable when using only one data series

Add check mark to return reformatted charts to their default appearance

Chart sub-type appears above while its name and description appear below

Sets selected chart type as default type for subsequent charts

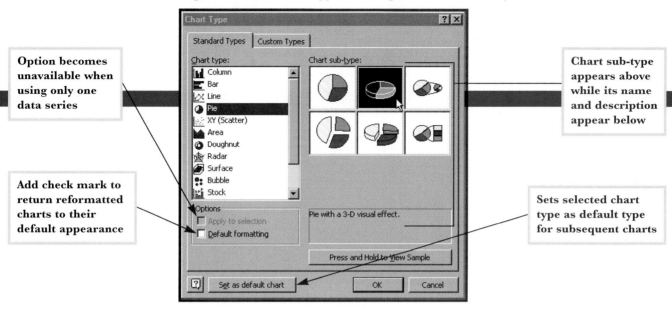

Figure 4-29 3-D View dialog box

Click respective arrow to increase or decrease chart elevation by 5-degree increments

Type value to increase or decrease elevation by 1-degree intervals

Enter value or click buttons to rotate chart around vertical axis

Returns dialog box to default format settings

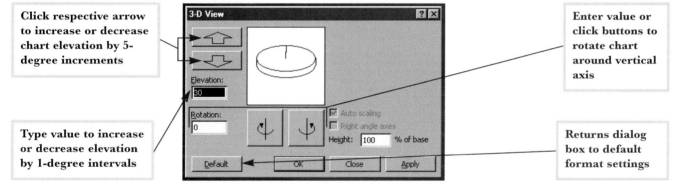

Figure 4-30 Chart with 3-D effect and increased elevation

Font, font style, font size, and data percentages remain the same

3-D pie chart elevated to 30 degrees above horizontal

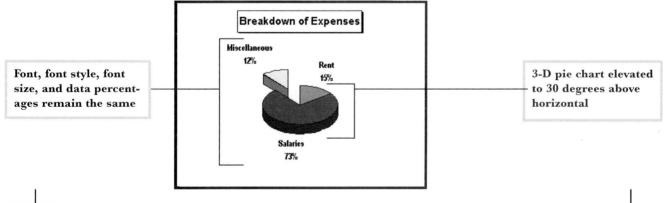

Practice

To practice changing a chart's type, follow the instructions on the Practice4-8 Sheet tab of the practice file exprac4.xls. Save changes as myexprac4-8.xls and close the file.

skill Using Advanced Printing Features

concept

A worksheet, especially one with an embedded object like a chart, may not always fit on a standard printed page using the default print settings. Excel therefore enables you to preview and change page orientation to accommodate different arrangements of data. You can choose to print specific parts of a worksheet such as a chart, a page, the active worksheet, or the entire workbook. You access these options through the Page Setup dialog box and the Print dialog box. Using these dialog boxes along with Print Preview will enable you to produce the kinds of printouts you need.

do it !

Change page orientation from Portrait to Landscape to fit an entire worksheet onto one page.

1. Open Student File exdoit4-9.xls and save it as Advanced Printing.xls. Replace the author's name in call B5 with your own name. Click the Print Preview button 🔍 to open the Print Preview mode. Notice that the worksheet and chart fit on one page in Portrait orientation. Click the Close button ⎡ Close ⎤ to return to Normal view.

2. Click once on the Chart Area. Hold down the [Alt] key and drag the chart up and to the right so the upper-left corner of the chart lines up with the upper-left corner of cell H2. Release [Alt], and click in cell G1. The chart now appears to the right of its related worksheet with one blank column between it and the worksheet's right column.

3. Click the Print Preview button 🔍 again. The documentation and data areas of the worksheet will appear on the page, but the chart will not, making it apparent that not all of the worksheet fits on one page. ⬛ Notice that the Next button on the Print Preview toolbar is active, that the words Preview: Page 1 of 2 appear in the Status bar, and that the raised area of the Vertical scroll bar goes only halfway down the bar. These are additional indicators that your worksheet spreads over two pages (see Figure 4-31).

4. Click the Setup button ⎡ Setup... ⎤ to open the Page Setup dialog box. Click the Page tab to move it to the front of the dialog box. In the Orientation section of the dialog box, click the Landscape option button. In the Scaling section click the Fit to 1 page(s) wide by 1 tall option button (see Figure 4-32).

5. Click the Margins tab to bring it to the front of the dialog box. In the Center on page section, apply a check mark to the Horizontally check box. This action will center the worksheet and chart equally distant from the left and right margins (see Figure 4-33). Press [Enter] to apply the page setups and to close the dialog box. The entire worksheet with the chart now appear on one page (see Figure 4-34).

6. On the Print Preview toolbar, click the Print button ⎡ Print... ⎤ to open the Print dialog box. Then click ⎡ OK ⎤ to print the worksheet and chart.

7. Click on the chart to select just it for printing. Click the Print button 🖨. The chart will print on one page. Save and close the workbook with the changes you have made.

more

The Header/Footer tab of the Page Setup dialog box contains default headers and footers to apply to your pages and options for setting up customized headers and footers. The Sheet tab contains options for selecting print areas, adding sheet titles, printing worksheet gridlines, and selecting other related features.

Figure 4-31 Worksheet's layout before applying page setups

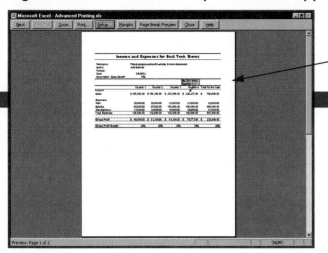

> Portrait page orientation; worksheet documentation and data areas appear; chart does not display

Figure 4-32 Page tab

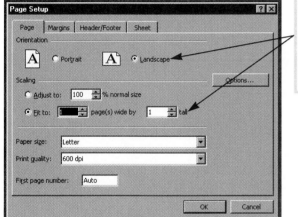

> Selected settings will put all print areas on one page in Landscape orientation

Figure 4-33 Margins tab

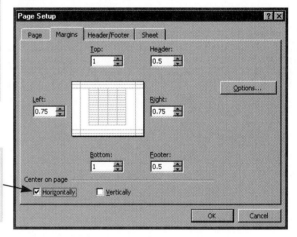

> Click here to center all print areas on a page

Figure 4-34 Worksheet's layout after applying page setups

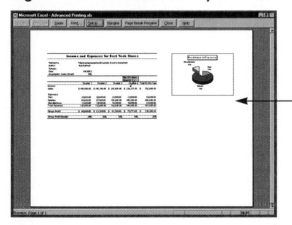

> Print layout changes to landscape orientation; chart displays to right of worksheet; areas to print are centered between left and right margins on page

Practice

To practice using advanced printing features, follow the instructions on the Practice4-9 Sheet tab of the practice file exprac4.xls. Save changes as myexprac4-9.xls and close the file.

shortcuts

Function	Button/Mouse	Menu	Keyboard
Drawing Toolbar		Click View, click Toolbars, click Drawing	[Alt]+[V], [T], then select Drawing
Text Box			
Arrow			
Fill Color			
Line Color			
Chart Wizard		Click Insert, click Chart	

A. Identify Key Features

Name the items indicated by callouts in Figure 4-35.

Figure 4-35 Identify features of the Excel screen

1. _____

2. _____

3. _____

4. _____

5. _____

6. _____

7. _____

8. _____

9. _____

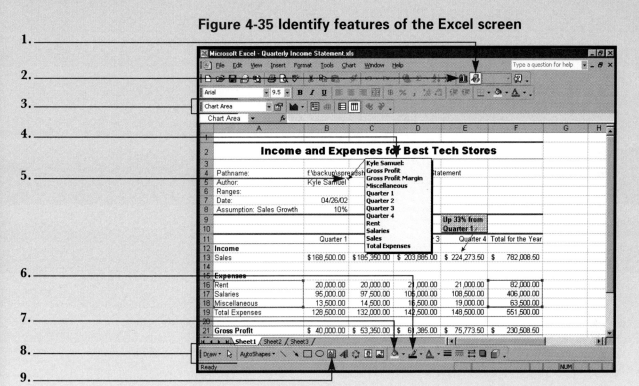

B. Select the Best Answer

10.	Allows you to add text to a worksheet without being restricted to a specific cell	**a.** Collapse dialog button
11.	Reduces the size of a dialog box so you can easily view a worksheet	**b.** Comment
12.	Displays with your chart when you complete and close the Chart Wizard	**c.** Drawing toolbar
13.	An electronic note attached to a cell	**d.** Text box
14.	A graphic that represents values and their relationships from a worksheet	**e.** Reviewing toolbar
15.	Alternate term for horizontal page orientation of a worksheet	**f.** Landscape
16.	Enables you to add text boxes, arrows, lines, and so on to a worksheet	**g.** Chart toolbar
17.	Applies shading to a text box	**h.** Fill Color button
18.	Contains Show Comment, Edit Comment, Delete Comment, and similar buttons	**i.** Chart

quiz (continued)

C. Complete the Statement

19. To change the user name that appears on Comments, go to the:

    a. Replace dialog box

    b. Define Name dialog box

    c. General tab of the Options dialog box

    d. User tab of the Comments dialog box

20. The Arrow tool appears on the:

    a. Formatting toolbar

    b. Define Diagrams toolbar

    c. Drawing toolbar

    d. Shapes toolbar

21. To navigate from one Comment to another, use the:

    a. Comments toolbar

    b. Reviewing toolbar

    c. Formatting toolbar

    d. Standard toolbar

22. Excel contains all of the following chart types **except**:

    a. Doughnut

    b. Line

    c. Pie

    d. Volume

23. You can add a title to a chart by using the:

    a. Chart Options dialog box

    b. Chart type dialog box

    c. Format Chart Area dialog box

    d. Source Data dialog box

24. To maintain a chart's center point when resizing it:

    a. Press [Ctrl] while dragging the chart

    b. Press [Ctrl] while dragging a sizing handle

    c. Press [Shift] while dragging a sizing handle

    d. Press [Tab] while dragging a sizing handle

25. The 3-D View dialog box contains all options **except**:

    a. Elevation

    b. Height

    c. Location

    d. Rotation

26. If text in a text box exceeds the size of the box:

    a. The beginning of the text will be deleted

    b. The excess text will be deleted

    c. The text box automatically will resize itself

    d. The text will scroll up

27. The small circles at the corners and the middle of each side of a selected object are called:

    a. Fill handles

    b. Frame handles

    c. Sizing handles

    d. Format handles

28. Text boxes can contain:

    a. Text in words, phrases, or sentences

    b. Individual numbers or a series of numbers

    c. Currency and mathematical symbols

    d. All of the above

interactivity

Build Your Skills

1. Add objects and graphics to a worksheet:

   a. Open the file exskills4.xls and save it as QIS with Chart.xls.

   b. Using the Drawing toolbar, add a text box in cells E9:E10 that reads Up 37% from Quarter 1. Use the Fill Color button to add a Light Turquoise color to the text box.

   c. Draw an arrow from the lower-right area of the text box to the top center of the Quarter 4 Gross Sales cell (E13). Use the Line Color button to change the color of the arrow to Dark Teal.

   d. In cell B6, enter the name Kyle Samuel in an alphabetized Comment that displays the names of all 12 cell ranges in the worksheet. (Hint: you can view the names of the cell ranges by clicking Insert, Name, and then Define.)

2. Create a chart based on the expenses data of the worksheet:

   a. Select the four values of expenses that appear in the worksheet (cells F16:F19). Use the Chart Wizard to create a basic pie chart showing the percentage of each expense as a part of the total expenses.

   b. In Step 2 of the wizard, use the Series tab to select the appropriate Category Labels (cells A16:A19).

   c. In Step 3 add the chart title Expenses by Category; leave the Legend displayed at the right side of the chart, and show Percentage data labels.

   d. In Step 4 insert the chart into the current worksheet.

3. Move, resize, and format the chart:

   a. Move the chart so that it is centered below the data portion of the worksheet. Using the [Alt] key, position the top border of the chart at the boundary of rows 25 and 26. Position the left border at the boundary of columns A and B. Position the right border at the boundary of columns E and F. Position the bottom border at the boundary of rows 40 and 41.

   b. Change the chart's sub-type to a 3-D Exploded Pie. Increase the Elevation of the pie to 60 degrees. Rotate it 20 degrees counterclockwise so the Rotation text box reads 340.

   c. Change the color of the Phone/Utilities pie wedge to Dark Green. Add a double underline to the chart title.

4. Save and print the worksheet:

   a. Type your name in an appropriate cell and resave the file. Print the worksheet and chart in Portrait orientation.

   b. Move the chart on the worksheet to position the top border of the chart at the boundary rows 1 and 2, the left border at the boundary of columns G and H, the right border at the boundary of columns L and M, and the bottom border at the boundary of rows 15 and 16.

   c. Using Print Preview and the Setup button, select the Landscape orientation and Fit to 1 page options on the Page tab. Select the Center on page horizontally option on the Margins tab. Close the dialog box and reprint the worksheet and chart on one page.

   d. Click on the chart to select just it. Add your name to the chart title and then print the chart on one page. Resave and close the worksheet with the changes you have made.

interactivity (continued)

Problem Solving Exercises

1. Use Excel to create the worksheet and chart below. You will need to use the Drawing toolbar and the Chart command or Chart toolbar to reformat the chart once it is created. When you finish formatting the chart, add categories and data for the months of July through December. Reformat the chart as needed to make all areas of it readable, organized, and attractive. Add your name to a text box in the upper-left corner of the chart. Save the chart as Web Hits.xls, and print the worksheet and chart on one page for your instructor.

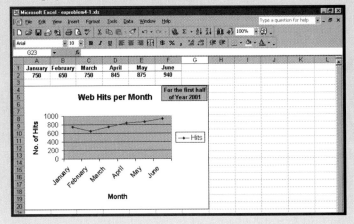

2. A friend of yours is considering learning Microsoft Excel. You want to convince your friend that the goal is worthwhile. To do this, you plan to show him or her a worksheet you have created with Excel. First, however, you decide to incorporate the Skills you have learned in this lesson to demonstrate the charting features of the program. Open the file exproblem4-2.xls and save it as Chart Features.xls. Add at least one text box, one comment, and a 3-D clustered column chart to the worksheet, using these new features to call attention to and further illustrate important data in the worksheet. Add your name to an appropriate cell, then resave and print the worksheet and chart on one page for your instructor.

3. You are training a new payroll clerk to use your school or company payroll worksheet, but you first want to modify the worksheet to make it more informative for the clerk. Open file exproblem4-3.xls and save it as Payroll with Chart.xls. Insert a text box to indicate that the clerk should type in new employee names with the last name first, then a comma, and then the first name. Add a comment to list your name and the cell range names for every column of the worksheet. Create a 3-D, exploded pie chart to show what percentage of the gross pay total is represented by the totals of the deductions and the net pay. Add your name to an appropriate cell, then resave and print the worksheet and chart on one page for your instructor.

4. Using the data in the table below, create and save a worksheet and 3-D stacked area chart with the file name Federal Taxes.xls. (If you add a Totals row at the bottom of the worksheet, do not select it when creating the chart.) Label the chart Internal Revenue Collections. Label the Y axis as Dollar Amount (in thousands). Label the X axis as Tax Year. The Legend categories should read Corporate, Individual, Employment, and Miscellaneous. Make additional formatting changes as needed so the chart looks organized, attractive, and readable. Add your name to an appropriate cell, then resave and print the worksheet and chart on one page for your instructor.

Internal Revenue Collections, Fiscal Years 1998-2001 (in thousands of dollars)				
Type of Tax	1998	1999	2000	2001
Corporation income tax	213,270,012	217,582,369	216,231,412	222,434,643
Individual income tax	928,065,857	1,003,185,952	1,000,587,123	1,150,425,581
Employment taxes	557,799,193	567,456,321	639,540,537	680,411,209
Miscellaneous	92,564,665	86,971,505	95,863,963	120,569,788

glossary

 a

Absolute cell reference

A cell reference that will remain fixed, even if the formula containing the reference is moved. To make a cell reference absolute, place a dollar sign ($), before both the column letter and row number.

Active cell

The currently selected cell on a worksheet, indicated by the cell pointer.

Alignment

The position of values or labels within a cell (for example, left, right, or center) in relation to the cell borders.

Anchor cells

The first and last cells in a cell range; the cells used to express a range address (for example, B9:E9).

Animated border

Indicates that a cell's contents have been sent to the Clipboard.

Answer Wizard tab

A Help tab that allows you to ask questions about Excel topics, much like the Office Assistant.

Argument

Information such as a cell address, range, or value, enclosed in parentheses, used by a function or macro to produce a result.

Arithmetic operators

Symbols used by Excel to perform formula calculations such as +,−,*, and /.

Assumption

A variable factor that is useful for conducting What-If analysis in a worksheet.

AutoCalculate box

Automatically displays the total of the values in a selected group of cells in the status bar.

AutoComplete

Automatically finishes entering a label when its first letter(s) match that of a label used previously in the column.

AutoFill

Automatically fills a range with series information such as the days of the week when the range after the first value is selected using the fill handle.

AutoFormat

Adds a predesigned set of formatting to selected ranges. AutoFormats can modify numbers, borders, fonts, patterns, alignment, and the height and width of rows and columns.

AutoSum

A function that automatically adds the values in the cells directly above or to the left of the active cell.

 c

Cancel button

Removes the contents of a cell and restores the cell's previous contents if there were any; marked by an X on the Formula bar.

Cell

The space formed by the intersection of a row and a column; the basic unit of a worksheet.

Cell address

A cell's identification code, composed of the letter and number of the column and row that intersect to form the cell (for example, B22).

Cell pointer

The black rectangle that outlines the active cell.

Cell reference

An address used to refer to a cell in a formula such as E11. Cell references can be relative or absolute.

Chart

A graphic representation of values and their relationships, used to identify trends and contrasts in data.

Chart Wizard

A series of specialized dialog boxes that guide you through the creation or modification of a chart.

Check box

A small square box that allows you to turn a dialog box option on or off by clicking it.

Clipboard

A temporary storage area for cut or copied text or graphics. You can paste the contents of the Clipboard into any cell, worksheet, or even another application file. The Windows Clipboard holds a piece of information until it is replaced by another piece of data, or until the computer is shut down. The Office Clipboard holds up to 24 pieces of data at once and can be viewed in the application window as a Task Pane.

Close

To quit an application and remove its window from the screen. You can also close a file while leaving the application open. The Close button appears in the upper-right corner of the application or worksheet window.

Column selector button

The gray rectangle that appears above each column and displays its column letter.

Comment

An electronic note that can be attached to a cell. Similar to a text box, but can be hidden from view.

Contents tab

A Help tab that organizes Excel's help files by topics and subtopics, much like the table of contents in a book or an outline.

Control menu

Contains commands relating to resizing, moving, and closing a window.

Copy

To place a duplicate of a file, or portion thereof, on the Clipboard to be pasted in another location.

Cut

To remove a file, or a portion of a file, and place it on the Clipboard.

Data series

The selected data taken from a worksheet and converted into a chart.

Delete

To remove the contents from a cell or an object such as a chart from the worksheet.

Dialog box

A box that offers additional command options for you to review or change before executing the command.

Documentation

The first section of a worksheet. It contains important information such as the spreadsheet's author, purpose, date of creation, file name, macros, and ranges.

Drawing toolbar

Contains tools for creating and formatting shapes, text boxes, and WordArt.

Dummy row/column

A blank row or column at the end of a defined range that holds a place so that Excel can recalculate formulas correctly if a new row or column is added to the range.

Edit

To add, delete, or modify cell contents or other elements of a file.

Electronic spreadsheet application

A computer program designed to organize information in columns and rows on a worksheet and facilitate performing rapid and accurate calculations on groups of interrelated numbers.

Ellipsis

Three dots (...) after a command that indicate a dialog box will follow with options for executing the command.

Enter button

Confirms cell entries. The Enter button is located on the Formula bar and is symbolized by a check mark.

Exploded pie slice

A pie chart slice that has been dragged away from the rest of the pie to emphasize it.

f

Fill handle

The small black square at the bottom right corner of the cell pointer. Draging the fill handle copies a cell's contents to adjacent cells or fills a range with series information.

Floating toolbar

A toolbar housed in its own window rather than along an edge of a window. Toolbars in Excel 2002 can be dragged to a floating position.

Folders

Subdivisions of a disk that function as a filing system to help you organize files.

Font

A name given to a collection of text characters of a certain size, weight, and style. Font has become synonymous with typeface. Arial and Times New Roman are examples of font names.

Format

The way information appears on a page. To format means to change the appearance of data without changing its content.

Formula

A combination of cell addresses and operators that instructs Excel to perform calculations such as adding, subtracting, multiplying, or averaging.

Formula bar

The area below the Formatting toolbar that displays cell contents whether they are labels, values, or formulas. You may enter and edit cell contents in the formula bar rather than in the cell itself.

Function

A built-in formula included in Excel that makes it easy for you to perform common calculations.

Go To

A useful command for moving great distances across a worksheet.

Gridlines

Vertical and horizontal lines on a chart that delineate a cell's boundaries.

i

Index

A Help tab that lists all of Excel's help topics alphabetically.

Input

The data you enter into a worksheet and work with to produce results.

Insertion point

A vertical blinking line on the screen that indicates where text and graphics will be inserted. The insertion point also indicates where an action will begin.

l

Label

Text or numbers that describe the data you place in rows and columns. Labels should be entered in a worksheet first to define the rows and columns and are automatically left-aligned by Excel.

Label prefix

A typed character that marks an entry as a label. For example, if you type an apostrophe before a number, it will be treated as label rather than as a value.

Landscape

A term used to refer to horizontal page orientation; opposite of "portrait," or vertical, orientation.

Launch

To start a program so you can work with it.

Legend

The section of a chart that details which colors or patterns on a chart represent which information.

Macro

A set of instructions that automates a specific multistep task that you perform frequently, reducing the process to one command.

Menu

A list of related application commands.

Menu bar

Lists the names of menus containing application commands. Click a menu name on the menu bar to display its list of commands.

Merge and Center command

Combines two or more adjacent cells into a single cell and places the contents of the upper left-most cell at the center of the new cell.

Mouse pointer

The usually arrow-shaped cursor on the screen that you control by guiding the mouse on your desk. You use the mouse pointer to select items, drag objects, choose commands, and start or exit programs. The shape of the mouse pointer can change depending on the task being executed.

Name box

The box at the left end of the Formula bar that displays the address of the active cell or the name of a selected range that has been defined and named. You can also use the drop-down arrow in the Name Box to select a named range.

Object

An item such as a chart or graphic that that can be relocated and resized independently of the structure of the worksheet.

Office Assistant

An animated representation of the Microsoft Office 2000 help facility. The Office Assistant provides hints, instructions, and a convenient interface between the user and Excel's various help features.

Open

Command used to access a file that has already been created and saved on disk.

Order of operations

The order Excel follows when calculating formulas with multiple operations: (1) exponents, (2) multiplication and division from left to right, (3) addition and subtraction from left to right. In addition, operations inside parentheses are calculated first, using the above order.

Output

The results produced by calculations done on the input data of a worksheet.

p

Paste

To insert cut or copied data into other cells, worksheets, or workbooks.

Paste Function command

Command that allows you to choose and perform a calculation without entering its formula on the keyboard.

Paste Special command

Allows you to paste the contents of a cell using formatting characteristics that you specify.

Personal Macro Workbook

Allows you to store macros so that they will be available to all Excel workbooks.

Point size

A measurement used for the size of text characters and row height. There are 72 points in 1 inch.

Portrait

A term used to refer to vertical page orientation; opposite of "landscape," or horizontal, orientation.

Print Preview

Allows you to view your worksheet as it will appear when printed on a sheet of paper.

Program

A software application that performs specific tasks, such as Microsoft Word or Microsoft Excel.

Programs menu

A menu on the Windows 95 or 98 Start menu that lists the applications on your computer such as Microsoft Excel.

r

Radio button

A small circular button in a dialog box that allows you to select one option in a set of options.

RAM (random access memory)

The memory that programs use to function while the computer is on. When you shut down the computer, all information in RAM is lost.

Range

A group of two or more cells, usually adjacent.

Range name

A name chosen for a selected group of cells that describes the data they contain.

Relative cell reference

Allows a formula to be moved to a new location on a worksheet. The formula will then follow the same directional instructions from the new starting point using new cell references.

Reviewing toolbar

Contains commands for inserting, deleting, displaying, and navigating between comments.

Right-click

To click the right mouse button; often used to access specialized menus and shortcuts.

Row height

The measurement of a cell from top to bottom.

Row selector button

The gray rectangle that appears to the left of each row and displays its row number.

Run

To start an application. Also refers to initiating the steps of a macro.

s

Save

Stores changes you have made to a file maintaining the file's current name and location.

Save As

Command used to save a new file for the first time or to create a duplicate copy of a file that has already been saved.

ScreenTip

A brief explanation of a button or object that appears when the mouse pointer is paused over it. Other ScreenTips are accessed by using the What's This? feature on the Help menu or by clicking the question mark button in a dialog box.

Scroll bar

A graphical device for moving vertically and horizontally through a document with the mouse. Scroll bars are located along the right and bottom edges of the document window.

Scroll bar box

A small gray box located inside a scroll bar that indicates your current position relative to the rest of the document window. You can advance a scroll bar box by dragging it, clicking the scroll bar on either side of it, or by clicking the scroll arrows.

Sizing handles

Small circles or squares on the corners and sides of a selected object that can be used for changing its dimensions.

Select All button

The gray rectangle in the upper-left corner of the worksheet where the row and column headings meet. Clicking the Select All button highlights the entire worksheet.

Series of labels

A range of incremental labels created by entering the first label in the series and then dragging the fill handle the number of cells desired. Excel automatically enters the remaining labels in order.

Sheet

The term Excel uses to refer to an individual worksheet (Sheet 1, Sheet 2, etc.).

Sheet tab scrolling buttons

Allow you to access Sheet tabs that are not visible in the window. An Excel workbook opens with only 3 worksheets, but you may use 255 per workbook.

Smart tag

Enables you to perform external actions on types of data that Excel recognizes such as names, e-mail addresses, and Web addresses. Items with Smart Tags are underlined with purple dots on the screen.

Status bar

Displays information regarding your current activity in Excel such as when a cell is ready for editing and when the Number Lock is activated.

Start

To open an application for use.

Start button

A button on the taskbar that accesses a special menu that you use to start programs, find files, access Windows Help and more.

Taskbar

A bar, usually located at the bottom of the screen, that contains the Start button, shows which programs are running by displaying their program buttons, and shows the current time.

Task Pane

A new feature to Excel that organizes common Excel tasks in one pane that is convenient to access on the screen. Numerous Task Panes are available including New Workbook, Basic Search, and Clipboard.

Text box

A rectangular area in which text is added so that it may be manipulated independently of the rest of a document.

Title bar

The horizontal bar at the top of a window that displays the name of the document or application that appears in the window.

Toolbar

A graphical bar containing buttons that act as shortcuts for common commands.

Values

The numbers, formulas, and functions that Excel uses to perform calculations.

What-If analysis

Technique by which you change certain conditions in a worksheet to see how the changes affect the results of your spreadsheet output.

Window

A rectangular area on the screen in which you view and work on files.

Workbook

An Excel file made up of related worksheets. An individual workbook may contain up to 255 worksheets.

Worksheet

The workspace made up of columns and rows where you enter data to create an electronic spreadsheet.

Worksheet tab

The markers near the bottom of the window that identify which worksheet is currently active. To open a different worksheet, click its tab. Worksheet tabs can be named to reflect their contents and colored for organizational purposes.

X-axis label

A label summarizing the horizontal (x-axis) data on a chart.

Y-axis label

A label summarizing the vertical (y-axis) data on a chart.

index

a

Absolute cell references:
  defined EX 2.14
  using EX 2.16-2.17, 2.19
Addition, in formulas, EX 2.6-2.7, 2.18
Alignment, in cells
  horizontal, EX 3.3
  of labels, EX 1.14
  of values, EX 2.4
  vertical, EX 3.3
Animated borders, EX 2.2
Answer Wizard, in Help, EX 1.26
Apostrophe, for labels, EX 1.15, 2.4
Application window, features of, EX 1.6
Area chart type, EX 4.9, 4.12
Arguments, for formulas, EX 2.8, 2.9-2.13, 2.16
Arithmetical operators, EX 2.6-2.7, 2.18
Arrows, inserting in worksheets, EX 4.4-4.5
Ask a question box, EX 1.24
Assumptions, for worksheets, EX 1.2, 2.16-2.19
Auto Fill Options Smart Tag: see "Smart Tags"
AutoComplete, EX 1.15
AutoFill, EX 2.3, 2.12-2.13, 3.18-3.19
AutoFit, columns, EX 3.8
AutoFormat command, EX 3.20, 3.22-3.23
AutoFormat dialog box, EX 3.22-3.23
AutoRecover, EX 1.18
AutoShapes, EX 4.4
AutoSum, EX 2.8-2.9
AVERAGE function, EX 2.10-2.11

b

Bold button, EX 3.4, 3.22, 4.2, 4.4
Bolding:
  cell contents, EX 3.4-3.6
  text boxes, EX 4.4-4.5
Borders, adding, EX 3.22
Buttons, program: see "Control icons"

c

Cancel button, EX 1.14
Category axis names, EX 4.8
Cell pointer, EX 1.8-1.10

Cell references:
  absolute, EX 2.14, 2.16-2.19
  relative, EX 2.12-2.15
Cells:
  clearing contents of, EX 1.14, 2.16
  defined, EX 1.2, 1.8
  editing, EX 1.22-1.23
  indenting contents, EX 3.4
  locking and unlocking, EX 3.14
  merging and splitting, EX 3.2-3.3
Center button, EX 3.4
Chart data series names, EX 4.8
Chart sheets, EX 4.8
Chart, EX 4.12-4.13, 4.16-4.17
Chart Wizard:
  defined, EX 4.8
  using, EX 4.10-4.13
Charts:
  changing type of, EX 4.18-4.19
  creating, EX 4.10-4.13
  embedded, EX 4.8
  formatting, EX 4.16-4.17
  moving and resizing, EX 4.14-4.15
  printing, EX 4.20
  understanding, EX 4.8-4.9
Clicking, EX 1.4
Clicking and dragging, EX 1.4
Clipboard, Office, EX 2.2, 2.3
Close button, EX 1.6
Collapse dialog button, EX 4.10
Color palettes:
  Fill color, EX 4.4-4.5
  Font color, EX 3.4-3.5
  Line color, EX 4.4-4.5
  on Patterns tabs, EX 3.20-3.21, 4.16-4.17
Color, selecting:
  of arrows and text boxes, EX 4.4-4.5
  of cells, EX 3.20-3.21
  of chart elements, EX 4.16-4.17
  of fonts, EX 3.4-3.5
  of tabs, EX 1.12
Column chart type, EX 4.9, 4.12
Columns:
  default width, EX 3.9
  defined, EX 1.8
  formatting, EX 3.8-3.9
  hiding and unhiding, EX 3.12-3.15
  inserting and deleting, EX 3.10-3.11
  widening, EX 3.8-3.9
Comma style button, EX 3.6

Comma style, for values, EX 3.6
Comments:
  adding to worksheets, EX 4.6-4.7
  defined, EX 4.6
  editing, EX 4.6-4.7
  reviewing toolbar, EX 4.7
Context-sensitive menus, EX 4.4
Control icons, program, EX 1.6
Copy button, EX 2.12
Copying and pasting:
  formulas, EX 2.12-2.13
  labels, EX 2.2-2.4
Currency style button, EX 3.6
Currency style, for values, EX 3.6
Cutting and pasting labels, EX 2.2-2.3

d

Data markers, in charts, EX 4.8
Data series fill, EX 3.18
Decimal places, setting, EX 3.6-3.7
Define Name dialog box, EX 3.16
Defining and naming cell ranges, EX 3.16-3.17
Deleting:
  cell contents, EX 2.16
  rows and columns, EX 3.10-3.11
#DIV/0! error value, EX 3.10
Division, operator for, EX 2.6, 2.18
Documentation section, of worksheets, EX 1.2
Double-clicking, EX 1.4
Dragging and dropping:
  defined, EX 1.4
  to copy cell contents, EX 2.2
  to move cell contents, EX 2.2
Drawing toolbar, EX 4.2-4.3
Dummy columns and rows, EX 3.10-3.11

e

Editing cells, EX 1.22-1.23, 2.2-2.3, 2.16-2.19
Electronic spreadsheets, EX 1.1-1.3
Enter button, EX 1.14, 2.2, 2.6
Error values:
  #DIV/0!, EX 3.10
  #REF!, EX 3.11

Excel:
    exiting, EX 1.6, 1.28
    Help, EX 1.24-1.27
    screen, EX 1.4-1.13
    shortcut on Desktop, EX 1.4
    starting, EX 1.4-1.5
Expand dialog button, EX 4.10
Exponentiation, operator for, EX 2.6
Extension, file name, EX 1.3

f

File name extensions, EX 1.3, 1.20-1.21
Files:
    closing, EX 1.16-1.19
    opening, EX 1.20-1.21
Fill Color button, EX 3.20, 4.4
Fill handle, EX 2.3, 2.12-2.13, 3.18-3.19
Filling a cell range with labels, EX 3.18-3.19
Folders:
    create new, EX 1.16-1.19
    My Documents, EX 1.16
Font Color button, EX 3.4
Fonts, EX 3.4-3.5
Footers, entering: see "Header/Footer tab"
Format Cells dialog box, EX 3.4-3.6, 3.20
Format Painter button, EX 3.2
Format Text Box dialog box, EX 4.14
Formatting:
    cell contents, EX 3.4-3.6
    labels, EX 3.4-3.6
    text boxes, EX 4.4-4.5
    values, EX 3.6-3.7
    with AutoFormat, EX 3.22-3.23
Formatting toolbar, EX 1.6, 3.6-3.7
Formula bar, EX 1.22, 2.2, 2.6, 2.8, 2.10, 2.12, 3.16
Formulas:
    copying and pasting, EX 2.12-2.15
    copying with AutoFill, EX
    creating, EX 2.6-27
    deleting, EX 2.14-2.15
    using functions with, EX 2.8-2.11
    order of operations in, EX 2.18
Fractions style, for values, EX
Function Arguments dialog box, EX 2.10-2.11
Functions:
    and Insert Function dialog box, EX 2.10-2.11
    AVERAGE, EX 2.8, 2.10-2.11
    defined, EX 2.8
    SUM, EX 2.8-2.9

g

Gallery tab, EX 1.24
Go To dialog box, EX 1.12-1.13, 3.14
Gridlines:
    major and minor in charts, EX 4.8
    printing in worksheets, EX 2.20
Growth series fill, EX 3.18

h

Header/Footer tab, EX 4.20
Help System, Excel, EX 1.24-1.27
Hiding and unhiding rows and columns, EX 3.12-3.15
Horizontal scroll bar, EX 1.8

i

Increase Indent button, EX 3.4
Indenting cell contents, EX 3.4
Index, for Help topics, EX 1.26-1.27
Input, defined, EX 1.2
Input section of worksheet, EX 1.2
Insert Function feature, EX 2.10-2.11
Insert Options Smart Tag: see "Smart Tags"
Inserting:
    functions, EX 2.10-2.11
    rows and columns, EX 3.10-3.11
Italic button, EX 3.4
Italicizing:
    cell contents, EX 3.4
    rows (or columns), EX 3.8

l

Labels:
    creating, EX 1.14-1.15, 2.8-2.10
    defined, EX 1.14
    editing, EX 1.22-1.23
    filling a cell range with, EX 3.18-3.19
Landscape orientation, EX 4.20-4.21
Line chart type, EX 4.9, 4.12
Line Color button, EX 4.4
Linear series, EX 3.18
Locking and unlocking cells, EX 3.14

m

Macros, EX 1.2
Margins, setting, EX 4.20-4.21
Maximize button, EX 1.6

Menu bar, EX 1.6
Merge and center button, EX 3.4
Minimize button, EX 1.6
Mouse pointer, EX 1.10
Moving:
    and resizing charts, EX 4.14-4.15
    chart elements, EX 4.16-4.19
Multiplication, operator for, EX 2.6, 2.18
My documents folder, EX 1.16

n

Name, defined, EX 3.16
Name box, EX 1.8, 3.16-3.17
New button, EX 1.6
New Folder dialog box, EX 1.16-1.18
New Workbook task pane, EX 1.7
Numeric keypad, using when entering values, EX 2.4

o

Objects, moving and resizing, EX 4.14
Office Assistant, EX 1.24-1.25
Office Clipboard, EX 2.2-2.3
Office Clipboard task pane, EX 2.2-2.3
Open and Repair, EX 1.20
Open as Copy, EX 1.20
Open dialog box, EX 1.20-1.21
Open Read-Only, EX 1.20
Operations:
    defined, EX 2.18
    order of, in formulas, EX 2.18
Ordinals, EX 2.4
Output section of worksheet: see "Results section of worksheet"

p

Page Orientation:
    landscape, EX 4.20-4.21
    portrait, EX 2.20-2.21
Page Setup dialog box, EX 4.20-4.21
Paste Options Smart Tag: see "Smart Tags"
Pasting:
    copied formulas, EX 2.12-2.15
    copied labels, EX 2.2-2.3
    copied values, EX 2.4-2.5
    cut labels, EX 2.2-2.3
Percent Style button, EX 3.6, 3.10-3.11
Percent style for values, EX 3.6
Personalized menus, EX 1.6
Pie charts:
    changing to 3-D, EX 4.18-4.19
    creating, EX 4.10-4.13

elevating 3-D, EX
    formatting, EX 4.16-4.17
    moving and resizing, EX 4.14-4.15
    3-D, EX
Portrait orientation, EX 2.20-2.21
Print button, EX 2.20, 3.12, 4.20
Print Preview mode, EX 2.20, 4.20
Printing worksheets
    in landscape orientation, EX 4.20-4.21
    in portrait orientation, EX 2.20-2.21
Protect Sheet dialog box, EX 3.14
Protecting worksheets, EX 3.14

r

Ranges, cell, EX 1.2, 3.16
    defining and naming, 3.16-3.17
    filling with labels, EX 3.18-3.19
Redo button, EX 1.22
Reference text box, EX 1.12-1.13
#REF! error value, EX 3.11
Relative cell reference, EX 2.12-2.15
Resizing charts, EX 4.14-4.15
Results section of worksheet, EX 1.2
Restore button, EX 1.6
Reviewing toolbar, EX 4.6-4.7
Rows:
    changing height of, EX 3.8
    default height of, EX 3.9
    defined, EX 1.8
    formatting, EX 3.8-3.9
    hiding and unhiding, EX 3.12-3.15
    inserting and deleting, EX 3.10-3.11

s

Save As dialog box, EX 1.16-1.19
Saving and closing and workbook, EX
    1.14-1.18
ScreenTips:
    and button functions, EX 1.7
    and AutoFill, EX 3.18
    and charts, EX 4.8
    defined, EX 1.6 and 1.26
Scroll bars, EX 1.8-1.11
Searching for files, EX 1.20-1.21
Series dialog box, EX 3.18-3.19
Sheet tabs, EX 1.8-1.9, 1.12
Sheet tab scrolling buttons, EX 1.8-1.9,
    1.12
Shortcut/pop-up menus:
    and cutting, copying, and pasting labels
        and values, EX 2.4-2.5
    and hiding and unhiding rows and
        columns, EX 3.10-3.11

and inserting and deleting rows and
    columns, EX 3.12-3.13
    and tabs, 1.12
Shortcut, Excel on desktop, EX 1.4
Smart Tags:
    Auto Fill Options, EX 2.12-2.15, 3.18
    Insert Options, EX 3.10
    Paste Options, EX 2.12-2.13
Spreadsheets, electronic, EX 1.1-1.3
Standard toolbar, EX 1.6-1.7
Start button, EX 1.4
Status bar, EX 1.8-1.9, 2.6
Stock chart type, EX 4.12
Strikethrough font style, EX 3.5
Subtraction, in formulas, EX 2.6-2.7, 2.18
SUM function, EX 2.8-2.9
Subscript and superscript font styles, EX
    3.5

t

Tab scrolling buttons: see "Sheet tab
    scrolling buttons"
Tabs, sheet: see "Sheet tabs"
Task panes:
    New Workbook, EX 1.7
    Office Clipboard, EX 2.2-2.3
Taskbar, Windows: see "Windows Taskbar"
Text box button, EX 4.2
Text boxes, EX 4.2-4.3
3-D chart type, EX 4.18-4.19
Title bar, EX 1.6
Tool Tip, EX 2.8-2.9
Toolbars:
    activating/displaying, EX 1.6
    and View menu, EX 1.6
    Chart, EX 4.12-4.13, 4.16-4.17
    Drawing, EX 4.2-4.5
    Formatting, EX 1.6, 3.6-3.7
    Reviewing, EX 4.6-4.7
    Standard, EX 1.6-1.7

u

Underlining cell contents, EX 3.5
Undo button, EX 1.22

v

Values:
    defined, EX 2.4
    entering, EX 1.14, 2.4-2.5
Vertical scroll bar, EX 1.8

w

What-If Analysis, EX 1.2, 2.16-2.19
What's This command, EX 1.26
Windows Desktop, EX 1.4-1.5
Windows Taskbar, EX 1.4-1.5
Workbook, defined, EX 1.3
Worksheets:
    adding and editing comments in, EX
        4.6-4.7
    adding new, EX 1.12
    and AutoFormat, EX 3.22-3.23
    assumptions section in, EX 1.2
    closing, EX 1.16-1.19
    creating and editing charts in, EX 4.10-
        4.19
    documentation section in, EX 1.2
    input section in, EX 1.2
    moving around in, EX 1.10-1.13
    opening, EX 1.20-1.21
    printing in landscape orientation, EX
        4.20-4.21
    printing in portrait orientation, EX
        2.20-2.21
    protecting, EX 3.12-3.15
    results/output section, EX 1.2
    saving, EX 1.16-1.19
    text boxes in, EX 2.2-2.5
World Wide Web, searching via Excel, EX
    1.20
Wrapping text, in text boxes, EX 4.2

x

X axis, EX 4.8-4.9

y

Y axis, EX 4.8-4.9

z

Zoom box, EX 4.2

The table below summarizes the external data files that have been provided for the student. Many of the exercises in this book cannot be completed without these files. The files are distributed as part of the Instructor's Resource Kit and are also available for download at http://www.mhhe.com/it/cit/index.mhtml. Please note that the table below lists only the raw files that are provided, not the versions students are instructed to save after making changes to the raw files nor new files that the students themselves create.

Lesson	Skill Name/Page #	File Name	Introduced In
Lesson 1	Opening a Workbook/EX 1.20	exdoit1-7.xls	do it! step 4
	Opening a Workbook/EX 1.21	exprac1-7.xls	Practice
	Editing a Cell's Information/EX 1.22	exdoit1-8.xls	do it! step 1
	Editing a Cell's Information/EX 1.23	exprac1-8.xls	Practice
Lesson 2	Cutting, Copying, and Pasting Labels/EX 2.2	exdoit2-1.xls	do it! step 1
	Cutting, Copying, and Pasting Labels/EX 2.3	exprac2.xls	Practice
	Entering Values/EX 2.4	exdoit2-2.xls	do it! step 1
	Entering Values/EX 2.5	exprac2.xls	Practice
	Entering Formulas/EX 2.6	exdoit2-3.xls	do it! step 1
	Entering Formulas/EX 2.7	exprac2.xls	Practice
	Using Functions/EX 2.8	exdoit2-4.xls	do it! step 1
	Using Functions/EX 2.9	exprac2.xls	Practice
	Using the Insert Function Feature/EX 2.10	exdoit2-5.xls	do it! step 1
	Using the Insert Function Feature/EX 2.11	exprac2.xls	Practice
	Copying and Pasting Formulas/EX 2.12	exdoit2-6.xls	do it! step 1
	Copying and Pasting Formulas/EX 2.15	exprac2.xls	Practice
	Using What-If Analysis/EX 2.16	exdoit2-7.xls	do it! step 1
	Using What-If Analysis/EX 2.19	exprac2.xls	Practice
	Previewing and Printing a Worksheet/EX 2.20	exdoit2-8.xls	do it! step 1
	Previewing and Printing a Worksheet/EX 2.21	exprac2.xls	Practice
	Interactivity/EX 2.25	exskills2.xls	Build Your Skills #1
	Interactivity/EX 2.26	exproblem2-1.xls	Problem Solving #1
	Interactivity/EX 2.26	exproblem2-2.xls	Problem Solving #2
Lesson 3	Merging and Splitting Cells/EX 3.2	exdoit3-1.xls	do it! step 1
	Merging and Splitting Cells/EX 3.3	exprac3.xls	Practice
	Formatting Cell Labels/EX 3.4	exdoit3-2.xls	do it! step 1
	Formatting Cell Labels/EX 3.5	exprac3.xls	Practice
	Formatting Cell Values/EX 3.6	exdoit3-3.xls	do it! step 1
	Formatting Cell Values/EX 3.7	exprac3.xls	Practice
	Formatting Rows and Columns/EX 3.8	exdoit3-4.xls	do it! step 1
	Formatting Rows and Columns/EX 3.9	exprac3.xls	Practice
	Inserting and Deleting Rows and Columns/EX 3.10	exdoit3-5.xls	do it! step 1
	Inserting and Deleting Rows and Columns/EX 3.11	exprac3.xls	Practice
	Hiding, Unhiding, and Protecting Cells/EX 3.12	exdoit3-6.xls	do it! step 1
	Hiding, Unhiding, and Protecting Cells/EX 3.15	exprac3.xls	Practice
	Defining and Naming Ranges/EX 3.16	exdoit3-7.xls	do it! step 1
	Defining and Naming Ranges/EX 3.17	exprac3.xls	Practice
	Filling a Cell Range with Labels/EX 3.18	exdoit3-8.xls	do it! step 1
	Filling a Cell Range with Labels/EX 3.19	exprac3.xls	Practice
	Applying Shading, Patterns, and Borders to Cells & Ranges/EX 3.20	exdoit3-9.xls	do it! step 1
	Applying Shading, Patterns, and Borders to Cells & Ranges/EX 3.21	exprac3.xls	Practice

Lesson	Skill Name/Page #	File Name	Introduced In
Lesson 3	Applying AutoFormat to a Worksheet/EX 3.22	exdoit3-10.xls	do it! step 1
	Applying AutoFormat to a Worksheet/EX 3.23	exprac3.xls	Practice
	Interactivity/EX 3.27	exskills3.xls	Build Your Skills #1
	Interactivity/EX 3.28	exproblem3-1.xls	Problem Solving #3
Lesson 4	Inserting Text Objects/EX 4.2	exdoit4-1.xls	do it! step 1
	Inserting Text Objects/EX 4.3	exprac4.xls	Practice
	Enhancing Graphics/EX 4.4	exdoit4-2.xls	do it! step 1
	Enhancing Graphics/EX 4.5	exprac4.xls	Practice
	Adding and Editing Comments/EX 4.6	exdoit4-3.xls	do it! step 1
	Adding and Editing Comments/EX 4.7	exprac4.xls	Practice
	Creating a Chart/EX 4.10	exdoit4-5.xls	do it! step 1
	Creating a Chart/EX 4.13	exprac4.xls	Practice
	Moving and Resizing a Chart/EX 4.14	exdoit4-6.xls	do it! step 1
	Moving and Resizing a Chart/EX 4.15	exprac4.xls	Practice
	Formatting a Chart/EX 4.16	exdoit4-7.xls	do it! step 1
	Formatting a Chart/EX 4.17	exprac4.xls	Practice
	Changing a Chart's Type/EX 4.18	exdoit4-8.xls	do it! step 1
	Changing a Chart's Type/EX 4.19	exprac4.xls	Practice
	Using Advanced Printing Features/EX 4.20	exdoit4-9.xls	do it! step 1
	Using Advanced Printing Features/EX 4.21	exprac4.xls	Practice
	Interactivity/EX 4.25	exskills4.xls	Build Your Skills #1
	Interactivity/EX 4.26	exproblem4-2.xls	Problem Solving #2
	Interactivity/EX 4.26	exproblem4-3.xls	Problem Solving #3